THE EXPERIENCE OF ADOLESCENCE

THE
EXPERIENCE
OF
ADOLESCENCE

EDITED BY STEPHEN J. GOLBURGH
Northeastern University

SCHENKMAN PUBLISHING COMPANY, INC.

CAMBRIDGE, MASSACHUSETTS

For Linda

CONTENTS

Contents

PREFACE

Happy is the man that findeth wisdom,
And the man that obtaineth understanding.
Proverbs 3.13

MANY TEXTBOOKS dealing with adolescence explain only segments of the adolescent's behavior. In reading them, one rarely gets a picture of a real person. One learns something about people's intellectual changes over a period of years, or something about their physiology, or how they might be more scientifically studied. But the person is hardly visible. He is buried beneath charts, statistics, and intellectual and general conceptions.

The function of the psychology instructor is to help his students to understand a person, or, more specifically in this case, the adolescent person as a living, feeling, real, human individual. Yet we seem to get very few books that attempt to do this. One might ask why this is so. Perhaps some psychologists, being human, are fearful of whole people and their experiences and anxieties as they see and express them. Perhaps they are fearful because material of this sort arouses in them anxiety which makes them uncomfortable. Often they feel that this type of material is more than their students can tolerate, understand, or use effectively. So we have the results of tests, the questionnaires, the structured interviews, the experiments. We run our adolescent subjects through mazes, much as we run our rats, and we come up with "magic" numbers which we take to a chart and discover that something "significant" has been discovered.

In the material which follows, it is my intention to provide a "feeling" for the experience of adolescence. Intellectual explanations for behavior have an important place but can be overdone. We sometimes explain intellectually because it is too difficult for us to look, listen, and see emotionally.

We find it difficult to ask adolescents to tell us about themselves. What we do is ask them to tell us how they feel about Negroes, or sexuality, or how they feel about their mothers, brothers, fathers, or uncles. But we don't try to study them by asking them what really matters to them, or by setting the stage so that they can present us with this material in their own way.

This is not to say that case studies are not available. There are excellent ones. But there are also too many which are unnecessarily long, dull, overly scientific, pedantic, and highly structured. In studying such cases, we get so much information that we rarely know what it is that mattered to the person about whom the material was developed. Adolescents ought to be asked to tell us what they felt was important about their own experience in whatever way they want to present it. It doesn't seem particularly important how long, careful, complete, "scientific," or thorough such material is. What is important is that they be allowed to write about what really matters to them in their lives. I provided students in many classes in several universities, and over several years, the opportunity to let themselves go and to talk about whatever it was that they thought was important. Furthermore, I gave them my assurance that their identities would not be connected with the material. Such material is of value to the person who wants to gain a greater understanding of the psychology of the adolescent.

Many adolescents were willing to tell me of some of their inner feelings. They seemed to be able to forget about psychological terms and scientific methods, although they had studied a bit of psychology, and to talk mainly about their feelings in words that have meaning to them and to other people.

I received over a period of time two basically different types of productions. Some students seemed very able to talk about the kinds of things that exist within themselves which give one a real feeling for an individual—a truly personal document. On the other hand, some students instead wrote classical term papers. My feeling is that roughly one half of the students were able to allow themselves to produce "personal documents"; the other half found it necessary to write structured, intellectual research papers dealing with the subject matter of the course.

It might be suggested that those students who wrote "personal documents" wrote not what they felt, but rather what they thought the instructor wanted, or made up a story, a fantasy, about themselves. It was my impression, however, on studying the material, that this did not happen often, if at all. The reader must judge for himself.

On studying the "personal documents" one might come to the conclusion that these people were indeed abnormal, that they had significant emotional problems and took this opportunity to try to obtain temporary relief from these problems or ask for help. There may be some truth in this, and yet I strongly believe my subjects were essentially "normal" college students. A very few may have severe neuroses; fewer may be more seriously disturbed. The fact is, however, that these people were functioning well in the world in which they live: they were going to school, some while working; they have family to whom they are relating, boy friends and girl friends, and were and are in the very process of living life.

The scientist will ask me, and rightly so, about my population. My population comprised college students between the ages of approximately seventeen and twenty, i.e., the later adolescent stage. They were students in good, solid colleges, in most cases doing adequate, and in many cases well above adequate, academic work. I have more material to present on males than on females. Perhaps the reason for this is that inasmuch as I am a male, males found it easier to "let me in on their lives." Still, some women were able to do the same. These students were interested in many different areas of study—the arts, sciences, business, engineering, education.

My subjects were Catholics, Protestants, and Jews. Some were from wealthy families, others from poor families, still others from families at different levels throughout the range. Some were from the country and some from the city. Some had many brothers and sisters, and some were only children. Some had one or two siblings. Most probably had reasonably adequate parents and a few had highly inadequate ones. Some subjects were quite bright, others far less bright. Most had intact homes, though a few did not. They seem a fair sample of college students if one interprets this very generally. I have not provided this information for each person as I felt if it mattered to them, they would express it, and one of the tasks of the reader would be to try to understand their manner of doing this.

What I have to offer, with the permission of my students, whose identities are carefully concealed and guarded, is a series of experiences and thoughts which have been very important in their development as they felt and saw it. In presenting the material, I have done nothing to it, with the exception of cutting sentences to protect anonymity. It is mainly the "feeling" for adolescence that I wish to convey to the reader. Adolescence, like any period of life, seems to be a period of struggle. They suffer, they feel, they fight to survive, they fail, they succeed, and they end up on many steps on the ladder between "succeeding" and "failing."

My presentations are in no particular order. It would be very simple to present section headings, to talk about "identity," "aggression," "independence," "sexuality," "guilt"; and yet these seem so arbitrary to me that I simply have presented the material in the order that it fell into my hands.

I have not been so presumptuous as to attempt to explain or interpret this material. My personal theoretical orientation is based upon psychoanalytic psychology, but I believe there are other methods of attempting to understand and develop a feeling toward human experience, and I believe that instructors and students have the right to choose their own way of doing this.

This is not my material; it belongs to my subjects. They were good enough to loan it to me. In my study of adolescence in the college situation and in practicing psychotherapy with them, I have learned something which "everyone" supposedly knows. They have taught me, and I thank them for doing it gently, that they are human beings, and we can be of more value to them if we can look upon them not as cases, charts, numbers, correlations, labels, or parts of "controlled studies," but rather as people with thoughts, hopes, feelings, and anxieties, struggling to deal with themselves in what appears to be a very difficult world.

SECRETS IN SILLINESS

"The whole question of pledging and fraternity."

MY EYES GLOWED with an intense excitement. I was on alert to carry out the next command that would be bellowed at me. No matter how precisely I carried out the task, I would be wrong. My words meant nothing. I was as useless as shark's dung sunk 50,000 centimeters off the southernmost tip of Sicily. I was a rat, or, to put it in more explicit terms, I was a pledge of a college fraternity.

Once a psychologist and I were having a discussion on the merits and drawbacks of fraternity life. At that time, I was a pledge of a national fraternity. Twelve weeks later, I was a brother of the fraternity. The discussion between us was a give-and-take exchange. An ex-fraternity man himself, the Doctor was ranking out the myth of the college fraternity. As a pledge, I was defending as best I could the merits of fraternity, and the reasons why it was necessary. However, it would not be long until I would come to see the light in regard to what fraternity and brotherhood really meant. The best defense that I could come up with was what I had been told by the brothers. I harped on the theme that it was valuable.

As I am writing this paper, there is a constant conflict in my mind as to whether or not it is right for a fraternity man to rebel against the institution which he is supposed to value with a great deal of love. But obviously, if I am able to have these thoughts, they must be somewhere in my mind. I would imagine that I would be committing political suicide if this paper ever fell into the hands of some real gung-ho fraternity man. For I am running for office. It seems I'm a hypocrite, but yet I do feel as though I could straighten out the house, even if it does not entail a deep love for the fraternity. Plus, and I may as well be rational about the whole matter, the free room is worth the aggravation of this job.

1

If this report is going to be judged on English grammar, or any of the more conventional ways of grading a paper, then I am completely wiped out. I'm writing this as an exposé of what I presume to be my innermost feelings. The idea is to be free, and that is exactly what I intend to be. Now join me in my first pledge meeting, and continue to follow up until the present time (the writing of this paper).

The wood of the paddle had a stinging sensation as it was cracked upon my rear section. The first round consisted of six medium blows. After I gave the pledgemaster a flippant answer, I was again in "the position." Bent over, holding your "sac" with one hand, putting your other hand on your ankle, and prepared for the worst. The first meeting I had the misfortune of acting in my normal way. I was paddled fifteen times. A feeling of aggression toward the pledgemaster was building up with each belt of the paddle. I was so worked up, but yet I was helpless. I wanted to pledge, and would go through great discomfort to become a brother. Instead of striking the pledge-master after the paddling episode, I held down my aggression. I went upstairs after the meeting had ended and let out my emotion with a good long cry. I felt as though this was the behavior of a child. Perhaps it was. When I learned that I was not the only one to have reacted in this manner, I felt better. Knowing that someone else was sharing my misery made me feel as though the crying was normal. It gave me a feeling of relief.

That same night, my "big brother" came up to talk to me about fraternity, and how everything had a purpose. The purpose of the paddling was for respect. Then he went on to give me a real first-class selling job on what fraternity really was. I had thoughts of dropping out then and there, but my big brother convinced me of the merits of fraternity. I was sold. I would act with more respect and humility. I wanted fraternity, or so I thought. As the days turned into weeks, pledging became a part of me. I was residing in the fraternity house, so there was constantly the reminder that I was a pledge. The pledgemaster gave me and the rest of the pledges a beanie and a pledge pin. These were the symbols that advertised you were trying to become a member of the best fraternity on campus—so you were told. I was never without my pledge pin. I literally had it on my body 24 hours a day, 7 days a week. The threat of "God help the pledge who is caught without his pledge pin" kept ringing in my mind. The saying brought the pin in the shower and into the bed.

I tried to be what was considered a good pledge, while not having to rely on brown-nosing and being a yes man. It was hard for me to assume the yes man role. I was the type of person who was not afraid to speak out for or against something I believed in. Pledging put a restriction on my aggressive tendencies. Fortunately, I had control of them most of the time. A worker in my pledge class, I often stayed up late into the night doing some sort of task for the fraternity. However, I was wise enough to know my own capabilities, and if at any time school work was a pressing issue, I would simply tell the brothers that I had to study. They either liked it or lumped it. I kept on telling the brothers that I would be of no value to them if I were not in school. Most of the time the brothers showed wise judgment and gave me permission to study. If they did not, I would tell them where to go, brother or no brother. Naturally, I would have to make a formal apology to the brother, and ask forgiveness for my misbehavior. Oh, how humble can one get!

I was pleased to find out that during social functions, a pledge was on the same equal basis as a brother. This was really an accomplishment. Imagine, to be able to talk to a brother in a natural manner. No longer was there the invisible wall that separated the brother from the pledge. I could act myself. Well, at least as close to myself as I thought wise. There was always the thought in my mind that any actions which I might display that did not seem proper for a pledge would be brought up at the next pledge meeting. Therefore I had to act in a fairly disciplined manner. Never did I let myself fully unwind.

Everything has a purpose. Everything has a purpose. Everything has a purpose. Over and over, this statement was hammered into my head. If a brother told me to count the windows in the Y.M.C.A., I was supposed to believe that this would bring me closer to the meaning of fraternity. They told me that many of my pledge tasks would seem as though they didn't have a purpose, but that they really did, believe it or not. If you were disrespectful enough to ask the purpose, you knew that you were asking for trouble. I could not accept some of the beating-around-the-bush answers to questions.

The weeks rolled by. The numbers of the pledge class were rapidly depleting. Most of the pledges who dropped either could not take the mental and physical hazing, or they were having trouble in school. The fraternity dropped a few more, for they were not the proper image of the type of person that should represent their fraternity—if that means anything. All told, thirteen pledges left the ranks. Finally, I received the letter from the fraternity informing me that the brotherhood had taken a vote, and I had been ACCEPTED. This should have been one of the happiest days in my life. But somehow I was more relieved than happy. My happiness was of a subdued nature. After twelve weeks of a memorable ordeal, the fraternity accepted me. I belonged!

I now became disillusioned. Had I done the right thing in pledging in the first place? Was this really what I wanted? Sure, I had made many close friends, but friends had always been easy for me to make. Perhaps the entire episode was a waste of time and energy. There were times of enjoyment, but I could also have enjoyed myself without the fraternity. Did I join because I was not secure in my own thinking of what I really wanted out of life? All of these questions wandered around in my mind. I would answer these questions in time, as long as I kept an open mind and thought for myself.

The initiation program to me was unimpressive. I was never one for ceremonies and secret vows, and this was no exception. I witnessed (when not blindfolded) the entire solemn affair with a grain of salt. After the initiation to brotherhood ceremony was over, the secret meeting that I had always envisioned was about to get under way. The brothers surrounding me told me the first meeting would really impress me. It did not.

I went to bed that night wondering if I had not made a mistake by pledging. The pledge policy I thought was foolish. Now that I was a brother and had therefore attained my goal, I was disappointed. The invisible wall was no longer present. People acted like people did everywhere. The brotherhood I had wanted so much had its faults, just like any other group of people. Cliques that I was unaware of as a pledge came to the surface in a short time. Some brothers did not even associate with other brothers. But still, the fraternity went along, living in its made-up utopia.

Perhaps the greatest shock that I received in the fraternity meeting was when some of my pledge brothers were brought up for brotherhood. To me it was the most fruitless scene I had witnessed in a long time. Brothers who had nothing to say held the floor for long, boring periods of time, rambling on about how a particular pledge was unworthy of HIS fraternity. These brothers knew the pledge only as a pledge, not as the real person he really was. It is impossible to judge a person on an equal basis when you feel that he is below you. The brothers have this superiority feeling. I suppose that everyone likes to feel superior. But the way they picked apart the individual limb from limb was really upsetting. I couldn't believe what I was hearing. I imagined how the discussion went when I was brought up for brotherhood. After a three-hour marathon on a pledge who had pledged 14 weeks, the final vote ended up with a blackball. My stomach turned with disgust.

These were now my fraternity brothers and my fraternity, yet I felt as though I wanted no part of it. But I had obligated myself to the fraternity both monetarily and socially. Many of my closest friends were in my pledge class. I would now have to act like the other brothers in trying to establish the fact that certain pledges were ready for brotherhood. I now started to question the idea of whether there was any difference between a close friend and a brother. I concluded that the only distinction between the two was that the brother had a fraternity oath that was supposed to bind him to all other brothers. Once again I wondered.

Why are some people so interested in fraternity? Each year the new pledge class is larger. I assume that the prospective pledges have heard stories of what it means to be a pledge, yet they still come in droves, anxiously waiting to be made complete asses of. There certainly must be a strong inner drive in each pledge which helps him absorb all the guff that is handed out.

Perhaps they think, as did I, that the fraternity is some sort of utopia, where things are just too good to be true. Everything he has ever dreamed or heard of, and things that he wanted to be a part of—girls, booze, parties, friends—would be at his fingertips. He must hope to be a silver spoke in the great golden wheel.

I notice in the present pledge class the inner struggle of the individual to want to belong to my secret fraternity. These pledges do not know what is behind the wall (perhaps if they did, they would not pledge), yet they will put up with all types of ridiculous tasks and hazing. Once they are on the other side of the wall, a few, like myself, may give time to ponder the whole question of pledging and fraternity itself.

There comes a time in the life of a pledge when he goes through a series of asinine ordeals, devised by the most frustrated brothers, and in a capsule it is called hell night, or week, depending upon the amount of sadism in the group. The period of ordeal is supposed to make or break the pledge. I do not take part in these "horror shows." The older brothers told me it would make the pledge have more respect for the fraternity, while he was pledging. If anything, it has the opposite result. The purpose behind hell week, in my view, is to allow the frustrations of certain brothers to be taken out on the innocent pledge. It reminded me of the behavior of uncivilized, let alone unsophisticated, children, not grown men in college.

To the pledges of the new class, I have an attitude that most of the brothers do not reflect. I believe that if the individual wants the fraternity and meets some of its qualifications (obviously I have become a little particular without even realizing it), then let the person in.

So, we have seen my progress and reactions from pledge, to brother, to the writing of this paper. What will likely happen is that I will play the fraternity game for a year or two, and then I may have enough courage to admit to myself that I was kidding myself. The possibilities that my attitude toward the ideals of fraternity, as I understand them today, might change seem slight. The experience which I gained in this adventure has helped me to have a better insight into the thoughts and behavior of other people. This in itself is priceless knowledge.

WHEN 3 EQUALS 9

The impact of an accidental pregnancy

WHEN MY WIFE and I were married, we had just turned nineteen. At the time of our marriage, she was six months pregnant. She was working and living at home with her parents. I had just finished the first term of my sophomore year at college and was living at home. Up until two weeks before we were married, no one knew that she was pregnant. Everyone in our home town thought we were the couple that never engaged in any sexual activity other than maybe necking. There were many people who were quite surprised when word traveled along the grapevine of the town.

Because of what I had always heard from my parents, teachers, and priests concerning sex and teenagers, and because of the position I was in, I had many experiences, before and since my marriage, that created a great deal of tension and anxiety for me. These occurred in everyday interactions.

I didn't know how to tell people that I was getting married and my wife was pregnant.

Would they think that it could have happened to them? Would they think it was normal sex behavior for a young couple to have intercourse, and because they didn't realize fully what they were doing and the consequences of their actions, that the girl might get pregnant? Would they react as if there were something unusual about the whole thing? Would they think that I was something dirty and all I had ever done was take a girl into the woods to see how much I could get? Would my friends make fun of me because I "knocked up" a girl? If I was walking down the street toward another person, would he cross the street to avoid me because I was a dirty person? There were so many things I would ask myself. Maybe some would turn out to be true and maybe some were foolish, but I still couldn't help but ask myself these questions many times.

There were two people whom I wanted to tell that I was getting married before someone else told them. They were my principal and science teacher in high school. I had known them for some time and had always been able to go to either one for advice when I needed it. I knew they would be surprised, since I had just started school. I thought they might be a little disappointed at the thought of my wife being pregnant at the time of my marriage, but I was quite sure they wouldn't call me a bum and tell me not to bother them.

They reacted pretty much as I had expected them to. They knew it was too late for lectures on what not to do and they both wanted to help me. Both of them told me to come to them if I needed money for tuition or to buy the baby a pair of shoes.

They pointed out to me that I would find out who my real friends were. These would be the people who would have the same feelings toward me as they always had. On the other hand, there would be people who would change their attitudes toward me. I now think that people who react this way in this situation are very foolish and ignorant. I found that there are people who changed their attitudes toward me and there are those who haven't, such as these two high school people. I consider them to be very good friends, for they gave me moral support when I most needed it and they would do so again if it ever became necessary.

So far I haven't found anyone who has changed his attitude toward me directly because of my getting married and already having my wife pregnant. I am still friendly with everyone, but we don't have the same interests or the same things in common.

I think this is because I have someone else to spend my time with, and don't have the time to do any of the things that a single man does. Many of my friends still like to go drinking five miles from nowhere and get stinking drunk. My attitude toward this, since I have been married, is a little different from theirs. But I don't worry too much about the relationship I have with them.

I was married on a Wednesday night and had to return to school the next day. I didn't want anybody at school to know that I was married. I would take my wedding ring off before I got to school and put it in my pocket, and when I got out of school I would put it back on. This was a ridiculous and very immature thing to do, but nevertheless I did it.

A good question to ask myself now is, "Why didn't I want anyone to know that I was married?" Was it because everyone thinks that nineteen is too young for a person to get married, especially in the middle of his second year of college? The only reason a person in this position would get married is if he got his girl friend pregnant. Maybe I didn't want them to know that this was why I was getting married now, while in such an insecure position, instead of waiting four or five years.

Nobody at school knew that I was getting married and I was afraid of the questions that they would ask. I didn't know how I would answer them. Should I come right out and tell them why? Or should I tell them it is none of their business? Or that I got married for the same reasons as everybody else?

Another question that I can ask is, "Why was I afraid to say that my wife was already pregnant and we were just married?"

Society says that a couple is not supposed to engage in intercourse until they are married. The church says the same thing. I had heard this all my life. That it was the wrong thing to do as well as an evil and sinful act. Because I had always heard that it was sinful and evil to do these things, and even a worse thing to be found out or exposed by a premarital pregnancy, I considered myself an evil person and didn't want to be thought of as such a person by my peers and professors.

After two weeks of not wearing my ring at school, I finally began to wear it. One day before class I met several students I knew well. One of the boys said he heard that I had just gotten married. I broke out in a sweat and my legs felt a little weak. This was the first time that anyone had mentioned it to me. I was almost afraid of them and I wanted to run away before they could say anything else. I said that I had been married for a couple of weeks and showed them the wedding ring, which was on the hand I had just taken from my pocket. They didn't ask any more questions in regard to this, but I felt as if they were trying to figure out why I had gotten married all of a sudden and had never mentioned it.

I was quite relieved when they left. I walked into the classroom with another boy who also asked me if I was married. I didn't know him any better than I did anybody else in school and he didn't know me very well. But I told him that I was married and my wife was already pregnant. It didn't even bother me to tell him. Why, I don't know. Could it have been that I felt guilty about being married and no one knowing about it and I wanted to tell someone? Maybe I wanted him to know so he could tell the rest and I wouldn't worry about them not knowing that my wife was pregnant. If they knew, maybe they wouldn't put me in an awkward position by asking me questions.

Why should I worry about whether or not the other boys know that my wife is pregnant? Many of them could get a girl pregnant or have intercourse with many girls but are just not as unfortunate.

One day I was sitting in a classroom with three of the boys who didn't know I was married. They were talking about all their troubles and how much they had to worry about. I thought to myself that they think they have a lot of troubles, so I told them that I was married. They all looked at me with surprised faces. One of them asked if my wife worked and I said no, that she was pregnant and couldn't work. Word soon got around that I was married and my wife was expecting and I was relieved that everyone now knew what I didn't want to have to tell them. When my son was born I was very happy and proud as any new father is. I still felt funny when talking to someone and telling them I was married and had a child. I was afraid they would ask how long I had been married and what they would think when I told them three months.

I didn't come to school the day my son was born and I couldn't help but wonder how the boys at school would react the next day. I didn't see why they should react any differently to me than to anyone else who had just become a father, but I still thought about it.

The next day I went back to school and for the next couple of days just about everyone congratulated me. It didn't make any difference to them how long I had been married, at least it seemed that way.

I couldn't wait to tell my friends at home. It didn't bother me to talk to these people. They had always reacted toward me after I was married the same as before.

For the next several months I was always nervous if I told someone that I was married and a father. Most people would ask how long I had been married and how old my child was. I felt that they would be counting months to see if everything added up. I don't imagine everyone that I talked to added up the months because they probably didn't care, but I still felt awfully uncomfortable with some people.

Now that I have been married for several years and my child is growing up, I don't feel the same tension as I did.

I recently went for an interview for a job. During the interview the employer asked me how long I had been married, so I told him. He then asked how old my child was and I answered him without hesitation. Then I thought to myself, maybe he's doing a little arithmetic, and if he is, and he doesn't like it, I know what he can do with it.

I didn't get the job but I know, or hope, that his arithmetic, if he did any, had no bearing on his decision.

As I have just said, my attitude concerning what other people think of me with regard to my marriage has changed. I think that this change can be attributed to several things.

I first decided that it was none of anyone's business but mine. I'm the one that got married and I'm the one that has to support my family, and I'm the one that still has to go to school, and I'm the one that has to worry about these things.

If a teenage couple get married and the girl is pregnant, all anybody can do is accept it. When I say anybody, I mean parents, clergymen, and anybody that knows the couple. It may be a little hard for some people to accept if they want to think that things like this don't happen, and if they do happen, it is to someone they don't know.

When I went to my priest to tell him I wanted to get married, he asked me why I had waited for six months to reach this decision. All I said was that I was afraid. I didn't really know what I was afraid of, but I was afraid. He told me I was afraid of reality and that I had to face up to it.

I think this is why you have to accept something such as this. Once it happens, you have to face up to it. It is real and you can't say, "Hold it, I made a mistake so I'll erase it and start over again."

THE NATIONAL GUARD

Dependence—independence conflict

INDEPENDENCE IS PROBABLY THE MOST friction-riddled area between parents and adolescents. If the adolescent continues to live at home after high school, complications arise. While the adolescent who goes to work after high school can assert his right to independence, the college student has a more difficult time of it. The working adolescent generally pays for his own clothes, has his own car, and perhaps contributes to the home; therefore, he feels no guilt about demanding more independence from his parents, and his parents, while they would still like him to be dependent on them, realize that with his own income he can move out if not satisfied with the amount of independence granted. The move toward independence in this case is more easily accomplished.

The college student is another matter, however. He wants the independence his more mature status calls for; after all, the college atmosphere encourages him to think for himself and to express his own opinions. But he is still financially dependent on his parents, who are paying for his education. He feels an obligation toward them even though he feels entitled to independence from them.

I know from experience both attitudes. When I was graduated from high school, I had no intention of going on to college. I was out working and when restrictions which I felt were unreasonable were imposed, I rebelled. My threats to move into an apartment with some friends, while an open fight and while hurting both me and my parents, had the saving grace of clearing the air and resulting in my acquisition of more independence. I was free to take several trips without the traditional third degree parents like to impose, and my hours weren't as strictly regulated. My parents insisted on some authority because I was still living under their roof and they wanted some say in the life I was having.

When you're a girl (especially when you're going out in your own car at night), this can give a feeling of security. If anything should happen to the car and I was stranded, I knew that they would come to the rescue soon. One instance is this: I went out saying I would be back before one. A standing "joke" was, "If I'm not in by one, call out the National Guard." This particular night, while I was driving home, my car suddenly just died. I didn't have to start walking with my girl friend or accept help from passersby whom the newspapers had given me reason to be wary of. We just waited and a police cruiser came by. I called home from the station and was "rescued." But I knew that even if the cruiser hadn't come by, my father would have. Or maybe he would have called out the National Guard. (It might have been more fun.)

But back to independence and me. On the whole, I was fairly independent even though I was living at home. I had little trouble claiming the independence I wanted. What was probably more important to me now that I look back was that I didn't feel guilty about demanding my independence. I felt entitled to it and would fight to get it.

But things are different now that I'm at college. My parents are helping me pay for my tuition (no small sum); and even though I have a part-time job to pay for my clothes and gas, they are paying for the car and its insurance. I can't help but feel that I am a financial burden to them. They want me to continue in college and graduate; I know they want to be proud of me when I graduate (though sometimes I wonder if I ever will). They want to help me get through (my mother often laughs and claims she's working my way through college). I just wish I could do better at college, but I never did learn to study in high school and the time out of school really didn't strengthen my already poor habits. Perhaps if my grades were high, I wouldn't feel guilty about staying in college. But with usually average and occasionally better than and lower than average grades, I do feel guilty.

I have this unwarranted conviction that I am capable of doing superior work, but I don't know how. And if something doesn't come easily or if I have trouble comprehending it (like math in high school and economics here), I am too lazy to figure it out for myself. I want someone else to figure it out and then tell me so that I will know, but I don't want to struggle through with it myself. I know that this is a poor attitude and I'm defeating the purpose of education by not searching out the answers by myself, but with absolutely no interest in math or economics, I can't convince myself that it is important to me to learn them. In my favorite subject and major, English, I can sit and read for hours. To prove how much I like English, I can even reread it a dozen times without tiring of something like poetry (as long as it is good poetry). But in economics I can read it at the most twice and find my mind wandering and my eyes drooping. I tell myself to concentrate, that I need a good mark, but it is so tedious to me that I am finding myself doing very poorly in it. And then I feel guilty again.

How can I ask my parents to support my college costs when I don't feel that I deserve it? But, on the other hand, how can I disappoint them by dropping out or, even worse, failing? I'd like to do something for them by becoming someone that they can be proud of. But I don't know how to overcome my own laziness at applying myself to work. When issues come up at home that involve asserting a show of independence, therefore, I can't help but feel guilty. I'd like to say I'm going to try to do better at school and then I won't feel so guilty, but I will probably just go along the way I am, doing average work. When I graduate (see the confidence, not "if" I graduate), I will possibly get an apartment. But more likely I will stay at home and have the same kind of independence I had when I was working before.

I think that I basically like being dependently independent.

NOT THE SABBATH

Hostility, and other reactions to death

MY GRANDMOTHER lived with us during my adolescence. Since
she was a very devout Jew, it became necessary for everyone
in the household to follow suit so far as our religion was concerned. I therefore became a patriot of Judaism. I proceeded
to the synagogue every Friday evening to welcome the Sabbath
as well as every Saturday morning, to participate in the con-
duction of the services. This routine went on for three years, until
I was 12 years old. It was at this time that my mother became
very ill and was forced to be hospitalized. Being the youngest
in the family, I naturally was not told about her sickness, but
I would visit my mother at least twice a week. On these visits
there was no formal conversation carried on. There was a big
plastic tent around her bed and all one was able to do was to
wave, hopefully getting a return wave, and when I attended,
maybe even a smile. My visitations lasted no longer than ten to
fifteen minutes, when I would be immediately whisked out of
the room and be told to wait until the others had returned.

As the days went on, I could tell that something was wrong.
People were visiting the house and crying. My aunts and uncles
started to gather around the house, approaching me for absolutely no reason, patting me on the head, and telling me not to
worry, that everything would be all right . . . everything will be
fine. It was then that my grandmother came up to me and told
me to go to the synagogue and attend the Sabbath services.

It was on that Saturday, the day before Mother's Day, that I
began to proceed to the synagogue to fulfill my obligation to my
grandmother and to pray for Mom and attend the Sabbath
services. I used to enjoy attending Saturday services because of
a particular man who has long since passed away. His name was
Mr. Mayer. He was an elderly man of maybe seventy or seventy-
five years of age, but a very smart man. He somehow made me

17

feel comfortable and at ease, whereas I had always felt out of place with the other men, who always kept to themselves and had nothing to do with me. He would always surprise me by bringing me a piece of candy, which he would give me if I had done my lesson well for that day. He knew of the trouble in my household, and told me that he also was praying for my mother. When I told him about the plight in my home and of how everyone seemed concerned, he said, "Don't worry. God never takes anyone away on the Sabbath." I believed him, for, as I said before, he was a very wise man.

After the services, I received my candy from Mr. Mayer and ran home. I stayed in front of the house that afternoon and was just fooling around and playing, mostly cowboy games, with the other kids, when I suddenly heard my grandmother calling for me. I ran up the stairs and saw everybody in the corridor crying. It was a terrible and very uncomfortable atmosphere. My father and grandmother then told me to come out to the back porch. While walking down the hall, my grandmother started to cry and she fell to the floor, at which time everybody ran over to her. My father continued walking with me to the porch and told me in a somewhat broken up fashion that Ma had died.

It somehow did not ring a bell. I did not know what to do, nor how to react, as I had never experienced anything like this before. I did not know what was expected of me, nor what to expect. By this time, my father was on his knees in front of me, crying like a baby. Still not knowing what to do, I turned around, ignoring all the people still lined up in the hall, and went to my room and closed the door. The noise and crying was still going on outside and the only thing that I could remember was what Mr. Mayer had said—God never takes anyone away on a Sabbath.

My mother was only forty years old when she died. She was a good person and we had a lot of fun together. We never had a car, but somehow we managed always to go out on a Sunday afternoon ride with my aunt and her family. These thoughts and many others of this type were going through my mind like flashes as I sat in my room, looking out the window. During that whole time while my mother was in the hospital, it was not as if I would never see her again, for everyone told me that she was fine and would soon be home with us. My weekly visits, although only fifteen minutes in length, gave increased thoughts in my mind that she would surely be home, for I did not know at that time that a blood clot was speeding to her brain.

As time went by, people came into my room crying, rubbing their hands through my hair, messing it all up, and telling me not to worry. My aunts began covering all the mirrors in the house with towels and tablecloths, and in the living room a huge candle was lit. A Rabbi came into the room and told me that I would have to go to the synagogue every morning and every evening of every week for an entire year and say Kaddish. This is a mourner's prayer that the male children in a Jewish family say for the deceased parent, out of respect. I did not want to go because had it not been for my grandmother, I really wouldn't have wanted to go on Saturdays either, even less so now, because it was as though God had lied; for, in spite of what Mr. Mayer had said, He did take her away on the Sabbath. It was at this time during my life that I first started to ask the question "why." To this very day I still ask the question "why." You might call me an atheist if you wish.

I then was told to get dressed, as I would have to go to the funeral parlor that evening. In the Jewish religion, as soon as a death occurs, prayers are said, and the person is buried within a period of two days. After I had gotten dressed, time seemed to go by very slowly before we finally left for the funeral parlor. I had never been to a funeral parlor before. I had never seen a dead person before. It is true that we used to play games after seeing people in the movies getting killed, but it was somehow unreal now. In the movies, even at this age, we know that the star has not actually been killed and that even though he plays dead, he will be alive in real life. I could not visualize a real dead body. I can remember at that time trying to think about it, but at the same time trying not to, because it gave me the creeps.

My thoughts were quickly taken from me as it was finally time to leave. The consoling and mourning and the hands through my hair occurred over and over. Now it was beginning to be annoying. "Why don't they leave me alone, why don't they go home where they belong. I never see them anyway." People kept saying over and over again, "She was so young. She had everything to live for. She did not even see her son get Bar-Mitzvah." Every time they would mention the word Bar-Mitzvah, which is comparable to a confirmation, the screaming would get worse, and the people would run to me, shaking their heads and crying all the more.

We finally arrived at the funeral parlor. It was a small brick building with a huge awning that ran from the stairway all the way out to the street. When we entered, a host of men all attired in black approached us, and told us how sorry they were and not to worry because everything had been taken care of. These were the undertakers. These men immediately flew off into different directions, telling all the people congregated in the hallway to take their seats, for the mourning party had arrived. At the same time, another man, all dressed in black, told us to follow him. My brother, who is older than I, was crying hysterically while holding onto my hand; my father was standing behind me. We walked into a large room which had wooden benches on each side, as one sees in a church or synagogue. At the extreme end of the room was a platform with a huge coffin on top of it. To the right of the coffin was an elderly man with a long white beard, who kept rocking back and forth chanting prayers in a low monotone. We finally got to the front row and sat down. This same undertaker who led us down the aisle began to pin black ribbons on the clothing of each of the mourning party. The Rabbi then came forward and with a scissors cut the ribbon, while at the same time still chanting prayers. He then told us to go up and see my mother.

It did not look like her. She was so still and quiet and white. My hands were holding the side of the coffin, and it was only natural for me to reach out and touch her hand. I will never forget this as long as I live, for it was not the hand that I had known and that was so familiar to me. It was cold and clammy and unreal. The man in black told me not to touch her. In the meantime, my father and sister were still crying and, as if in unison, as soon as they began to cry, the other people in the room would cry, too.

I could not watch this any longer. I don't know why, but I ran back to the bench and began to cry more hysterically than anyone in the entire room. I could not control myself: I could not stop. Worst of all, I did not know what I was crying about. The only thing that I was sure about was that God had lied. Mr. Mayer had lied. I felt that there was no point in going to the synagogue and praying and that there was no point for this Jewish ceremony that we were having now. For the rest of that night, during the service, as well as during the service the following morning when she was buried, I never approached the coffin again to see my mother. I was asked to and I wanted to, for I loved her very much, but the mother that I had loved and the unreal thing that I saw in that coffin were not one and the same, and I could only wish that this experience would end as soon as possible.

For one year I went to the synagogue out of respect to my mother. As I said previously, there were two services daily. I attended both of them, one at 6:30 every morning and the other at 7:30 every evening, including Saturdays and Sundays. I did not want to go, nor did I believe in what I was doing and what I was saying, but because of respect and because everyone said that it was a wonderful thing that I was doing, I continued to attend faithfully.

Since that day, I have seen several people pass on. It was only a few months ago that a very close friend of mine was taken away at the age of 26, leaving a wife and child. When I attended his funeral, the Rabbi said during his eulogy that God had wanted him, that he had a purpose in mind for him, and that he was going away to a world far better than the present world in which we live. As soon as I heard this, I could only think of one thing. How foolish a man this Rabbi is! How foolish is anybody in this parlor who believes in what this man is preaching, for how can anybody console others by telling them to believe in something that he knows not from fact but merely from blind faith. How can anybody as good as he at 26 years of age, or as good as my mother at 40 years of age, be taken away with the excuse that someone by the name of God wanted them more than we here on earth do?

Sure, there must be a God—there must be a Supreme Being, but who are we, if there is a Supreme Being? Who are we as mere mortals to attach immortality to any Supreme Being and actually believe that there is a true so-called Garden of Eden in the hereafter that we will eventually end up in. It is my belief that all religions whether they be Christianity, Judaism, or what have you, are all a bunch of wishful thinkers. If there is a true God, whatever his title may be, how can he possibly stand by and watch six million people put to death in the most brutal manner which man can possibly devise. How can he possibly stand by idly and allow world war after world war to go on generation after generation, men killing men. How can this be true? Why is it that all miracles and everything else on this mumbo-jumbo line that we study in the Old Testament and the New Testament start and stop in the Bible?

During that period of my adolescence until the present day, I have constantly asked the question "why." To this day I am thoroughly convinced that there can only be one answer. Religion is a way in which a weak person can face the grim realities of life and death. Religion is a method in which man can find an escape to something that he knows nothing of, but fears. Religion is a means by which man can cope with fear through blind faith. I myself am afraid of death. I do not know of anyone who has returned from death to report on what death is. Death to me is distinguished by sorrow and through my experience, it is not something to be looked forward to. I do not know what death will bring me. I do know this: that in my present situation I do like life very much. Death to me takes me away from the life that I like and that I know. Death to me brings a fear of unknowingness which I panic thinking about. I cannot foresee any Almighty Being taking me away to live with him in a dreamed-up world of which I know nothing.

This event of my mother's death, along with the deaths of many people who were taken away from me and from this present world, has made me become a man without a faith in religion, and although this feeling does not coincide with modern thinking, I do not feel badly about it.

SHEILA MAKES
THREE AND A HALF

Adolescent anxiety about sex

WHEN ASKED TO CHOOSE a topic that is important to me, sex is the first subject to come to mind. While I have reservations about writing on this subject due to the amount of mixed emotions we place in a discussion of sex (humor, shame, etc.), I think I can handle it in an adult (if not scientific) fashion.

I will attempt, in this paper, to separate fact and fancy whenever possible. At times, however, these areas overlap in my mind and I will fail.

This discussion will be limited to two areas. I will include only heterosexual behavior except when other types are relevant to that. Likewise, I will limit the topic in span by only including preadolescence to the present.

Excuse me, paper, while I take a trip to the liquor cabinet. Enter: One large wine glass of Daddy's best liqueur. That'll teach him to sleep with my mother. (He doesn't any more—she snores.) I tell everybody that I can drink a pint of hard liquor before being drunk—I lie. It takes about a half a drink. Well, down to work.

I'm going to begin my story in my preadolescent peer group. I, however, was the only nonadolescent in it, or so it seemed at the time. I was younger than the others in my school class, so I was one of the last to notice the signs of incipient sexual maturity such as pigmented pubic hair (that wasn't because I wasn't looking, either). I was fairly large in physical size, however, and I had no problems in sports or being socially accepted. It was only in bull sessions about ejaculations and pubic hair that I felt really left out. My problem wasn't that I didn't know the score. I was probably the best informed in the bunch. It was just that I had no good stories to tell.

This was a minor problem for a while. I had no trouble attracting partners at "make-out" parties. I could talk about them on the school bus as well as anybody could. If it weren't for that god-damn Libby, everything would have been great. I still get a little excited when I think about that broad. Libby was about the best example of an early maturing girl that I ever heard of. She had a beautiful womanly body at twelve and made no secret of the fact that she was a nonvirgin. Libby was now the topic of every bull session. I didn't dare to go near her. Who could take his pants off in front of sophisticated Libby if he didn't even have hair on his "balls"? It seems that everybody in the back of the bus had at least been *played with* by Libby. All I ever did was feel her breast in a kissing game. Jimmy even claimed to have had intercourse with her. They went steady for a whole week. We all half believed him.

I was so damn inferior. My penis was too small. I was even ashamed to take a shower in gym (especially when my friend Chuck was there—he was big). I became very acutely aware of my other faults. I was too fat. I didn't even shave once a week. I didn't have one pimple. I dressed neatly. In short, I was a mess.

Well, it wasn't long until I did what I had to do. I became a *cat*. I grew a long D.A. hairdo. I wore tight dungarees (belt on the side, still do). I kept my collar up and my shirt unbuttoned to the navel. I started going steady with a girl with big breasts. In short, I was beautiful. I could now tell stories as good as anybody could (except Jimmy). Some of them were even true. "I wonder if I'm going to die a virgin," I remember saying. Even drinking large quantities of booze at friends' parties didn't seem to help. I was a good dancer, a funny storyteller, and everybody liked me, but I was to me an inferior person. My stories, as well formulated as they were, were big fat lies, and I knew it. (If I only had a penis like Chuck's.) I used to fight constantly with other guys, especially Chuck. He wouldn't even know the facts of life if I hadn't taught him.

The night I first ejaculated was beautiful. In my bed alone with visions of Susan dancing in my head I CAME. Chuck and I were best of friends that next day. Those short, barely black hairs would soon get longer and blacker, and I knew it. My stories in the bus became even more lurid and detailed. I was a man. My voice might even change. I might even get a pimple!

I soon had intercourse with Libby. Oops! Not really, but I spent an hour talking to her on her bed (about the Bible). She was in her sleeping gown, and that was enough to justify exotic yarns that would make D. H. Lawrence blush. "She said I hurt her," I related passionately, while everybody tried to hide their envy. Libby, wherever you are, I love you. No sexual intercourse ever gave the satisfaction that you gave me without your even knowing it.

I have had sexual intercourse with only three and one half girls in my life. (I'll explain that later.) If you asked any old friend of mine, however, he'll tell you that I was the most prolific lover since Byron—I lied quite a bit.

By the time I was fifteen I was tired of asking myself, "Will I die a virgin?" I answered it by spinning more and more tales of passion. I also read everything I could get my hands on about sex. I had to know: Was my penis average? What age do most boys start having intercourse? Where do those that do find them? Never once did right or wrong enter into my considerations. Everything is all right as long as you're careful. That is about as shallow as you can get, I guess.

Well, the next significant factor in my sex life is Judy. We were both juniors in high school, and we lived in neighboring towns. I met her at a party where she was pointed out to me as being promiscuous. I guess I wasn't the only boy to ever make up a story about a girl. We dated for two years, with heavy petting almost from the beginning. Each time we were tempted to go further I responded with, "No, Judy, I love you too much to hurt you." She always replied, "Phew!" Neither of us evidently wanted to get swallowed up. After two years of sexual frustration, we broke up because I thought that she had done "things" with other boys. Boy, I've always been jealous when it comes to my girl friends. We went back together again a few times, but it never worked out. Only one time was significant. Each time we resumed sexually where we had left off. Once I said, "Let's," and she said "Yes." I responded with a premature ejaculation in her vagina. This was a perfect climax to a frustrating sex life. We worried together for a month and parted. You should have heard the stories that she was good for! I was now only half a virgin, a demi-virge.

Then there was Nancy. This flat-chested, sexless, intellectual rebel kept me perfectly frustrated for three months. Half-hearted petting and fast driving of borrowed sports cars were my sex life for the whole time. I even masturbated once (or twice—or three times, or maybe—well . . .). She introduced me to Phyllis, though, before she moved to Arizona in a flood of tears.

Phyllis was sixteen, and I was a freshman in college. Sexually, she was much older than I. She was no virgin. She didn't do it for anybody as the rumor stated, but she had "been around." She just did it for love. It took her two dates to love me enough to confide that she had had intercourse once before and was sorry that she could not give me her virginity. I told her that I was no virgin either, and that I had "been around," too. For two years we were in love (or should I say in sex?). Together we fought the world, each other, and ourselves to be together. Our parents objected, my friends objected, and her other boy friends didn't like it either. For those two years we fought. I had my brains fastened squarely in my scrotum. I fought so hard I forgot to love or trust or enjoy. I just fought her. I was jealous and lonely. I just *knew* that it was me she really loved. It's still painful for me to think about her. I not only wanted her physically, but I desired the suffering we experienced together. It was a perfect atmosphere for the rebelling I was doing in religion and other intellectual areas. Finally, I cheated on her one drunken evening. It was her best girl friend. I couldn't look at Phyllis again.

I had sex with two and a half girls when I met wild but virginal Sheila.

She is young, attractive, tiny, and full of life. She thinks that she is great, yet hates herself. She is adopted and hates her mother but loves her cat and her father, in that order. Her parents are lovely and think a lot of me. Sheila is intelligent, lazy, moody, and lots of things. Most of all, she's screwed up. It took me two months to get this young screwed up thing to love me more than her cat by her own admission. I think she's great. I love her. She's just what I need until I grow up— a girl who needs me. Who knows, she might grow up with me.

I'm still jealous, still feel inferior, but I'm much happier than ever before sexually. Oh yes, Sheila makes three and a half.

NOT AN INCH

Difficulty with an "old country" father

I WAS AWAKENED that morning in the usual manner, by the call of "Angie! Angie!" in the hallway outside my bedroom. The fact that it was only 6:00 o'clock and I didn't have to get out of bed until 7:30 hardly made a difference, because this procedure hadn't been altered in the least for the past ten years. "All right," I screamed back, "I heard you the first time."

I dressed quickly, hoping to beat my father to the kitchen, knowing that the chances were very slim. I was right; as usual he was puttering around, whipping up his favorite breakfast treat, dropped eggs on toast. I just glared at him, not really knowing why, but just unwilling to break the tradition that I had set. No good mornings were exchanged. I just looked at the eggs and told him that I thought I'd prefer a boiled egg instead. This was not unusual, as I always had managed to do just the opposite of what my father did anyways.

"What kinda time did you get ina last night?" he asked.

"Early," I replied curtly.

"Whata ya mean early?"

His tone had reached a high pitch and I knew in a minute that he would be in a rage.

"This is not a homa to you!" he shouted, half in Italian and half in English. He always switched to Italian when he was angry because the words came easier to him.

"You call this a home?" I shouted. "Who wants to come home and hear you yelling all the time?" I pushed the plate away from me and stormed out of the room. "I'm not hungry now, anyway."

"I said eata that or elsa you'll never eata in this house again."

And so another delightful morning had passed.

On my way to school that day, I began to wonder why I found

27

it so hard to control myself when I was with my father. The reason could be that I knew he was right and didn't want to face up to it, or maybe I resented his old-country authoritarian manner toward me, when I knew I was old enough to be on my own.

He had always been somewhat of an authoritarian figure. He was the head of the household and what he said always went. In our home "children were seen and not heard," but the trouble with that was that I had never progressed further than the childhood stage in his eyes. Whenever I offered an opinion, it was always thought to be stupid or childish and never really considered of any value.

This attitude is reflected in my personality now. Although I am considered by most to be a very outgoing and forward person, I find it very hard to express an opinion outside of my own peer group, and always have the fear that my opinion might be looked upon as stupid.

This also works in the reverse. I very rarely accept an opinion of my father's and am always ready to argue about it even though I know he might be right.

Most amazing of all is that outside of my home I am a very different person. I'm usually pleasant to people I know and am considered by most to have a very even disposition.

The same can't be said about me when I'm at home. I no sooner step over the threshold, when my veneer changes and I become a bundle of nerves.

This situation is greatly contrasted when I am around my brother. His home is like an escape for me. When I am there I have no trouble saying what I feel, and know that my opinion will be respected. He also responds in the same way. Being older, he often feels that it is his duty to criticize me when he feels that it is necessary. I never react to his criticisms as I do to my father's. I usually accept them with the feeling that he is probably right. This is also true of any criticism I might receive from friends. I usually accept it without any feelings of resentment.

At school, too, I am a different person. I've often been told that I look so happy-go-lucky and don't appear to have a care in the world. Often I've wondered if I'm really as happy as I appear to be or is this just a mask I put on when I'm around other people. This could be the reason that I've always felt a strong need to be surrounded by friends. Innately there probably lies the fear that to be alone is to be without friends and consequently to be depressed.

The only question that remains is how to resolve these problems. How do you change a father from the old country who is set in his ways and who thinks that to budge an inch in your favor is to give up his authority? How do you control your temper, especially when you realize that a person is old? How do you gain enough confidence in yourself so that you can make a decision without the aid of ten people?

These are questions that may never be resolved, but at least the realization that these problems do exist is a step in the right direction.

LITTLE PLASTER MAN

Attaining relative maturity

I WAS BORN IN CANADA at which time my father was in Japan. My first year of life was spent with three women. These were my mother, older sister, and grandmother. Naturally, I was babied because all three waited on me hand and foot. According to child psychology, the first year is very important in determining how the child will see the world. I saw the world through a "milk bottle." My every need was fulfilled and I began to see the world as a nice place with nice people. At this time the war was still on, so most of the men were gone, leaving only women around the neighborhood. This meant even when taken out for a walk I came in contact with women. I heard, saw, and smelled nothing but women for the first year of my life. This sort of environment made me self-centered and all I had to do was cry and my wish was fulfilled. However, this abruptly changed when father returned from the service. He found me a spoiled brat and decided it was time to start making a man out of me. I remember when he first picked me up, I screamed bloody murder. I was scared to death, because he was the first man to touch me. The louder I screamed, the more he laughed and the more frightened I became. I began to hate all men and wanted only women to touch me. This was a natural outcome of being raised and pampered by women, and it was a long time before this fear subsided.

Two years later we moved to another town where I was to spend the next four years overcoming the fear of father. He was a carpenter and worked in a shop not far from home. Our home was a small bungalow located in a quiet part of town. The house had a small lawn in front with a little plaster man standing in the middle holding a fishing pole. At first glance the pole resembled a penis and we named the statue "Little Willie." The name scared me and for some reason I gave this name to my penis. I could never decide if I liked the statue or not. One day

31

I would and the next day I'd be scared to death even to look
at it. Possibly I saw father standing there with a large penis.

This can be related to being brought up by women. I am
assuming they didn't let me touch my genital organs because
they thought it wrong and therefore I thought touching or looking at Little Willie was wrong. My fear for this object was very
intense as was my fear of father. This fear kept building up and
when I was four years old I had a terrible experience concerning
Little Willie.

One day I awoke to find Willie trampled by a cow. I was
scared stiff and cried all day. I remember I didn't cry because
Willie was gone but because he was broken into pieces. I felt
this pain in my genital area and possibly I thought I would lose
my genitals now that Willie was gone. It took me a long time
to forget this and I was never sure if a cow or father had broken
him. I was always suspicious of father and this helped manifest
my fear of him.

I thought of father as someone who was out to get me. He
was a large man with a lot of strength and courage. He was
covered with hair and always dirty and sweaty from work. I
didn't like him because he was dirty and I was clean and neat.
He used to pick me up and rub his unshaven face against mine;
this not only hurt but enhanced my fear of him. I was close to
mother because I was used to women. I hated father because he
was receiving more love from mother. I saw him as someone
who wanted to destroy me and have mother all for himself.
I have often thought about this part of my childhood, but I
could never explain it.

It was a long time before I saw father as a nutrient person in
my life. It took only one episode for me to view father as someone who wanted and loved me.

One day I broke into a chicken pen and started beating the
chickens with a stick. While my back was turned a rooster
started biting the back of my knees. I had on short pants and
the rooster was making a mess of my leg. I screamed for help
and luckily enough father heard me. He rescued me from the
rooster and at this point I saw him as a totally different person.
He looked at my leg, patched it up, and sent me home. I realized
from this experience that father was someone who loved and

wanted me and could offer me protection. Now I wanted to be like father. I wanted to be like him not only to acquire the same amount of love from mother he received, but I wanted to be brave and strong. I wanted to get dirty and sweaty and wear old clothes.

At this point I would like to pick up a loose end concerning the chicken pen episode. Why was I beating the chickens in the first place? I believe this can best be explained by referring to the cow that trampled Willie. I became scared of cows and I started to despise them. Because a cow is an animal, I began to hate all animals. I saw them as poor creatures without brains. I could not take my hatred out on cows because they were too large, but chickens were small enough so they couldn't retaliate. I wanted to hurt the chickens the same way the cow had hurt me. I also mistreated our cat. One day I poured kerosene on his back and his back bent so much his stomach dragged on the ground. It gave me pleasure to see the cat squirm and twist with pain. As I think about it now, this might have had sexual connotation. Possibly I was a sadist and received sexual gratification by inflicting and witnessing pain. This explanation is of course only a thought and I believe a better explanation can be found in the relations with my parents. They were strict with me and possibly I wanted to treat animals the way I was treated. I resented the authority of my parents and decided I wanted authority also. Because I was too small to tell adults what to do, I believe I started to show animals I had some authority over them. This allowed me to release my aggression upon animals instead of people.

During the last two years in Canada there were no significant experiences that influenced my life. It was a small town and life there was not too demanding. There were no girls in my neighborhood, so I didn't have a chance to find out there was a difference between the sexes. I summarized there must be a difference because one day we went visiting some friends who had a girl. After playing for a while, she took off her pants but kept her skirt on. We continued to play for a while and then her mother came out. When she saw the pants on the ground, she made us stop playing together. This experience haunted my mind for a while and I was interested to find out what she had that I hadn't. I didn't want to ask father and after a short time I forgot about the whole affair.

I began to center my life around what father was doing. I liked to go places and do things with him. I wanted to act and think like him, and at the same time I didn't obey mother as much as father. I wanted him to tell me what I could and couldn't do.

I saw him as the perfect man and I wanted to be just like him. He was now planning to go to America and work there. I was now eight years old and the trip to the United States was a thrilling experience for me.

The drive to America was a great experience, but I didn't like the idea of leaving all my relatives. It gave me an insecure feeling, because I was leaving part of my family behind. I feel this experience helped strengthen my identification with father. He was the only man I knew in this country, so I looked to him for security and protection. We had a close family in comparison with American families. My parents were raised under old country discipline and so was I. Our new neighbors thought I was a perfect gentleman, the way I spoke and acted, but my new friends thought I was a sissy because I always obeyed my parents. This caused a great deal of anxiety, because I wanted to be one of them and at the same time my parents demanded that I follow their strict commands.

My social status among my peers became very low, even though I had a good identification with father. The reason for this can be attributed to the fact that father had different values than my peers. His values consisted of honesty, respect, courage, and hard work. He realized I was having trouble with my peers, so one day he told me, "If anyone calls you a chicken and you don't fight to disprove it, don't bother to come home again." This really shook me up, but it was all I needed to give me courage to stand up to my peers.

The following day I had a fight with one of the group's leaders. Although I was scared to death, I won the fight and eventually the respect of my peers. They accepted me into the group and this made me feel like someone. I began to see myself as a capable individual with confidence in myself and what I did. This helped me do better in school subjects and sports. I began to enjoy sports very much. As with every boy, my life centered around football. I loved the game, but father never played with me. He thought I was wasting my time. He never changed his views on sports and I feel this had a great influence on me in later life.

Up until the ninth grade, father and I were very close. We used to work together building things and remodeling the house. I used to help him with his job and we got along fine, until I asked him to go fishing or play ball. He kept telling me sports were a waste of time and I should spend more time working around the house. My favorite sport was football and my sophomore year I made the first string. This was a great achievement for me and I was very happy about it. All my friends and neighbors cheered me on, but I felt very lonely because father hardly ever went to watch me play. I became more withdrawn from him and at times it seemed I didn't know him. I felt lost and alone because the other boys' fathers were always at the games to watch them play. I started to become withdrawn from my friends because I was jealous of them.

My withdrawal from father and friends dealt a tremendous blow to my personality. In the lower grades I had a lot of fun and enjoyed being with people. I was group oriented. Everything the group did, I did with them. I was a leader and enjoyed the responsibility of making plans for parties and such. I was looked up to by my classmates for being a good athlete and student. All this changed when I started to withdraw from my friends. I was still considered a leader and during my junior and senior years in high school I was president of the class. This didn't change my personality, knowing people still looked up to me. I didn't act conceited or anything, but instead I became quiet and passive. I began to think for myself more and more. I didn't rely on anyone, not even Father, to help me with my problems. I went off by myself and thought about things and analyzed my problems by myself. I began to show resentment toward father for his lack of interest in school activities.

I showed this resentment by doing the opposite of what he told me to do. He wanted me to work, so I decided to loaf. He wanted me to join the service, so I decided to go to college. Everything he planned for me I did just the opposite. I hoped it would make him feel hurt if I thought for myself and in this way I could get back at him for hurting me. Although my personality changed greatly toward him, it didn't change too much toward my peers. I would like to give my explanation of a factor I think greatly influences a person's personality.

I feel a child's personality depends greatly on his parents' personalities. If his parents are quiet and passive, I believe the child will see these factors as something he should have. Using my parents as an example, I would like to see if their personalities are the same as mine.

Both parents are very quiet, passive, and easygoing. I feel this is attributed to their being foreigners. They never made any really close friends (friends they visited and went places with) in America. They kept to themselves and they wanted me to do the same. I feel they became jealous of my having so many friends. Possibly they thought they would lose me if they allowed me too much freedom and friends. I wanted to show them I still loved them, so I developed my personality like theirs in order to make them feel I wanted to be like them. This was a tremendous pressure on me and one day it was all released when I found out my mother was pregnant. I realized this would give me a chance to live my own life, because I knew they would have to spend much of their time with the new baby. This was what actually happened and I began to feel like a new person. Father stopped telling me what to do and I began to think more for myself. I was so happy gaining my freedom that I started to help around the house. I wanted to help because it was my own idea. No one told me what to do and this gave me a feeling of complete independence. I started to make my own dentist and doctor appointments and at first this really scared me. I could feel myself becoming very independent, but at the same time I felt insecure.

I believe this was the turning point of my life. Although it was a slow and painful transition, I went from complete dependence to complete independence. As I look back now, I believe this was the way father planned it. When I decided to enter college instead of the service, father didn't say anything about it. I knew he wanted me to go in the army and become a man, but when I asked him what he thought about my going to college, he said it was up to me. He said I'd have to make the decision myself, that he couldn't help me. Well, as you can see, I decided to go to college and I'm glad I did. I enjoy college very much and I'm working part time in order to put myself through. It's a great experience to realize you're on your own, and I can honestly say I wouldn't want it any other way. I am completely on my own and thinking for myself. I'm not easily influenced by other people and although I'm still not sure what I really want out of life, I feel I am quite capable of making the right decisions in order to reach the goals I have now set for myself.

In conclusion, as I look back on my life and see the things that influenced my present thinking and actions, I can see how easily I could have become a totally different person. If just one small episode had been changed, my whole personality might have turned out completely different from what it is now.

The experiences I have written about have been bothering me for a long time, but I never believed they could influence and shape my life the way they have. I thought these experiences were unique and could never happen to anyone else, but I realize now they are common to everyone in one way or another. I have realized I'm a normal person facing the same conflicts as everyone else traveling the long road to adulthood.

MORAL MOTHER

Peers, mother, and values

LAST WEEK I reached what society calls "the legal age." I am now considered mature enough to vote, to sign legal documents, to drink alcoholic beverages, and, in general, to be legally responsible for my own actions. By law I am no longer directly controlled by my parents nor are they responsible for my support.

Why do the lawmakers feel that I am suddenly capable of making my own decisions and of being socially responsible for them? Why, after exactly twenty-one years, do my parents lose control and responsibility? Why not after nineteen or even eighteen years?

It would be more reasonable to change "legal age" to "competent age" and offer a written examination to determine social capabilities. The twenty-one rule of thumb seems to hinder most present-day young adults rather than protect society from them. For example, in the presidential elections of 1960 and 1964, I, as well as my classmates, were more informed on the general issues than were our parents.

Between eighteen and twenty-one, most young adults make their own decisions and run their lives as much as possible. Although the restrictions of the law are not severe, they are a degrading hindrance to many. One feels that society does not consider him a responsible person when, in fact, he is.

Twenty-one is certainly not the age of great changes, physical or mental, but by this time, or before, the confusion of adolescence should have settled. The fully matured personality is now the result of a multitude of factors incurred in adolescence and before, both within and outside of the home.

For several days after my twenty-first birthday, friends whom I would meet would ask, "How does it feel to be twenty-one?" I kept wondering what they expected for an answer and why I was supposed to feel different than at any other birthday.

The answer is, of course, that society now recognizes that I am a responsible person. Society is like a parent, never willing to recognize the child's capability of independence. It is like a whole group of mothers and fathers acting as one, much like my own, sitting at the dining room table passing judgment on something I have asked permission to do.

What really does happen on a twenty-first birthday? Because of the emphasis put on this day, there is a significant difference. My mother, with her badly stretched apron strings, thinks I will become an alcoholic. This is rather strange, as I have had only three drinks in my whole life. The implication that there is more to this than at first appears is quite strong.

Mother has been an extremely dominant influence in my life, as my father was away much of the time during my childhood, but at home during my late adolescence.

It is interesting to note that most of my personality traits are adaptations of mother's personality. I often regret and rebel against this dominance, as I believe it has led me to be a very inhibited person.

Alcohol is an outstanding example of a mother-type inhibition. I have never seen mother take a drink, and the few times when father has had wine with dinner, she would not. When adults, on a social visit, would drink at my house, my sister and I were required to leave the room. After a party, mother would always comment that the way someone drank was disgusting. "Disgusting" . . . this is the attitude toward liquor that I was taught and one which I never questioned. Only recently have I decided that liquor isn't really so bad and shouldn't be eliminated entirely. However, I still cannot take a drink without feeling very guilty.

Another mother-type inhibition has been sexual activity. Just after I decided that God automatically gave only married women babies, my father, in a very mechanical way, told me about the "birds and bees." Later, I heard and half understood the gross ideas of my peers.

In my family, sex is a taboo subject. It is never mentioned in any manner of speaking. Although I never felt free to ask questions of my father, I can talk freely about sex with my peer group.

The suppression of any discussion on sex within the family had a considerable effect on my social adjustment with the opposite sex. I had fallen into the trap of many early-maturing boys. When I was taller and stronger than my peers, it was not necessary to strive for social acceptance; and when they caught up to and surpassed me physically, I faded into the background. It wasn't until my junior year in high school that I made an attempt to become socially reoriented. At this time I dated a girl for four months, but only held her hand once. Later in my senior year I dated another girl, who finally gave up and kissed me! Of course, I thought this was all very wrong and immoral, as I had been taught that kissing and lovemaking were only for those who were either married or in love, and I was neither. This didn't last long and soon many of these inhibitions began to dissolve. Today my sex life is probably equal to that of my peers; however, I still feel tremendous guilt when involved in necking or heavy petting.

Oddly enough, the use of profane language is another inhibition to which I am subject. Since mother never used profanity and taught me that it was sinful, I never used it. Although I accept the use of profanity by my peers, I often shudder to hear it.

If the word "inhibited" sounds a little regretful as it is used above, it is probably meant to be. The desire to engage in sexual activity, drinking, and even profanity exists within me, but so does a stronger conscience which says "no." It's a constant struggle between mother on one shoulder and a desire to conform with the peer group on the other. Although I am sure that the peer group is gradually winning, I know that "moral mother" will always be whispering in one ear while the peers are shouting in the other.

LAURA

Struggling to achieve sexual identity

LAURA STOOD STARING into the blackness. The night frightened her. She could see the houses, trees, and all the objects surrounding her take on a human-like image. She clutched her coat closer to her and quickly closed her eyes. She wanted all those things to leave her, to go away. She opened her icy black eyes in a flash, and dashed quickly down the street, up the stairs, as if someone were behind her, chasing her, and she dared not turn around. She had her key ready and opened the door in a swift movement, slamming it behind her. She was gasping, but still proceeded to turn on all the lights in the house. She always did this, as if to avoid some creature lurking in the barren blackness. Her mother would be angry and yell about her wasting electricity, but she was so frightened, and although she hated her mother screaming in that constant disapproving way, it was still better than the dark.

Laura went upstairs and lay dreamily on her bed. She was contemplative and lucid. She was afraid of many things in her life and felt that these all stemmed from fear of herself. She feared her own actions and projected them onto other situations. She felt guilty. Her whole life centered around seeking security and making herself feel less guilty. She felt any happiness she did receive was undeserved and she must suffer and punish herself. In a way, she looked for situations that would make her suffer. She lived in fear of rejection.

First, these feelings stemmed from her mother, who was the dominant factor in her family. Her sister Diane, a bit younger, was a more sedate individual and better adapted to her mother's highly excitable nature. Laura was like her mother in this respect and they clashed. But besides her mother's excitable nature, Laura had her father's casual, irresponsible look on life. Diane was responsible, like her mother. Laura's mother could not un-

43

derstand her casualness and carelessness, and praised Diane but chided Laura. Laura was jealous of Diane and reacted by being more sloppy and irresponsible. Laura's mother became constantly aggravated with her and asked her to try to be good like her sister. Laura couldn't be good like her sister. She was irresponsible and would never really be responsible, but because no matter how hard she tried, she could not consistently be what her mother wanted, she just began to feel defeated and no good. She felt guilty for not being like Diane, disappointed in herself, unloved, and inferior. Besides, her sister treated her in a protective, almost degrading manner. Her sister treated her like a little, irresponsible, foolish, lovable girl, and Laura began to live the role.

Her father was indulgent, but too much like Laura, so she could not talk to him. Besides, although he loved her, he only showed his love through material grants. Her brother was like Diane and her mother. But he only aggravated the situation and did not play a significant role in Laura's life.

Laura had always been drawn to mixed-up people. This made her feel superior. At twelve she formed a most significant relationship in her life. Laura was studying art and became friendly with a very dreamy, sad girl, Sheila. Sheila felt compelled to paint. When not painting if she wasn't with Laura she would often hear voices calling her and see images not real, and feel completely disjointed with the world. Sheila had had a nervous breakdown at 13, at least according to doctors. That year she lived more than ever in her own world; maybe she was schizophrenic. To everyone else, Sheila appeared very moody and always crying, but other than that, functionally normal. She seemed to be going through a severe crisis. Laura made Sheila happy. Laura was a girl of schemes and innovations, and found exciting things for Sheila to do with her. Sheila laughed with Laura, leaned on Laura for all the solutions to her problems. Laura was Sheila's only real tie with the world of reality, but Laura never revealed her true self to Sheila until very late in the relationship.

Although Sheila was jealous of time Laura spent with others, she depended too much on the relationship to curtail it. At 13, Laura slept at Sheila's house. They talked about their closeness and then began discussing a passage from Anne Frank that talked about touching another girl's breast. Sheila and Laura experimented. They touched each other all over. Sheila told Laura she had always felt a strong sexual drive. Laura asked her if she felt anything strange about their relationship, and Sheila answered that she felt most girls were not as close as they. She said any two people as close as she and Laura needed to express themselves physically, and it was natural for them. Laura and Sheila had both gone to all-girls' school and had no contact with boys. In her later years, Sheila switched to a co-ed high school, but the boys had no effect or part in her life. Laura remained in the girls' school because the academic training was good. Sheila couldn't take the pressure of that same school.

The physical relationship lasted a few years off and on, but Laura at age 15 decided to discontinue the physical relationship. Sheila wanted to continue but did not push Laura because their relationship was too good to lose. Everyone always joked about Sheila and Laura's closeness and talked about their getting married. Sheila liked the idea, but Laura thought it was absurd. After high school Sheila and Laura continued with their painting. Both went to college. Laura finally gave up art for a variety of reasons. With her extra time, Laura went into a great state of depression. She had been depressed all year about art lessons, realizing she was only taking them to become proficient in something. When she realized she would not be great, and that she had been struggling for nothing, she became depressed. She had other talents, but did not have the energy to go on. She felt a failure in her ambition, a failure in her social life, and a failure in college.

It was at this period that John came into her life. John was in his middle twenties, had been very upset emotionally when younger, was seeing a psychiatrist, and was having an affair with a married woman. John was sensitive to Laura and listened to her problems. John was insecure, but had gained a lot of strength in the last few years. He made Laura laugh, took her out, and made her feel appreciated. Laura knew about John from the beginning but did not seem to comprehend his situation. They saw each other constantly. Meanwhile, Laura's friends had given her a surprise birthday party. Sheila slept over. It had been four years since the end of their physical relationship. Sheila started holding Laura close to her. She touched Laura all over. Laura didn't do anything, but began to feel excited. Sheila went farther than ever before, wrapped her legs around Laura, and would have kissed her had not Laura suddenly started. She was shocked at herself and felt they both must surely be homosexual. She refused to see Sheila for a long time after that because of fear and doubt. Because of her doubts, she flaunted sex at John, but he always refused. Then one night Laura confessed to John. He comforted her and kissed her passionately, although they did not make love. John made Laura promise never to have any physical contact with Sheila.

The next time Laura saw Sheila was in the fall. She slept at Sheila's house and for the first time she reached a climax with Sheila. That seemed to end Laura's conflict. After that evening, she never had any physical relationship with Sheila. They were just friends. It seemed natural for it to end and Laura never slept at Sheila's again. John never knew about this final meeting. Their relationship had grown deeper emotionally and physically. Laura felt John's insecurity. He made everything of Laura and if things didn't always go well, seemed unhappy. Laura started becoming unhappy. They started an affair and Laura felt even more guilty. They were engaged. John was free of the other woman and completely devoted, yet Laura felt unfulfilled. Their physical relationship was good and she enjoyed making love. Somehow John wasn't all she wanted, yet because of her basic insecurity, her feeling that no one else would care for her the way John did, she was almost compelled to marry. Her parents didn't like the idea and therefore she fought for it more. Her wedding would be soon and she felt no joy, only a nothingness. Laura felt life was empty, devoid of happiness except for a few moments. She drifted into sleep, how peaceful, how wonderful its nothingness felt, oblivion at last.

NOT QUITE ANYWHERE

Conflict over ethnic background

THE "MARGINAL MAN" is the individual "who is part of a culture but not of it." This simple basic statement accurately describes my situation as a youth. My parents and ancestors were of purely Greek extraction, being firmly entrenched in the culture's customs and attitudes. I have attempted to be both a Greek and an American simultaneously; which I was more of at any given time depended on where I was and with whom. This is the core of my problem, which certainly is not unique.

Whenever possible, the Greek language was used in my home. As a youngster this brought me confusion no end. I can still remember the anger I felt when I couldn't make myself understood by my first playmates, at about age four.

In grades two to eight of primary school, my comprehension of language passed through the phases of understanding only Greek and no English, to understanding much English and very little Greek. During these years I had to attend Greek School, a parochial-like school held several times each week.

I experienced much anxiety as to how I could explain to my friends that my afternoons weren't free like theirs. Despite my efforts to be like them and still do as my parents wished, my peers saw me as somewhat of a "strange bird."

In retrospect, I now realize that I submitted to my parents' intense desires because of my youthful dependency on them. They firmly believed that the way they were raised was correct and their child would follow suit. There was many a "battle" on this specific point, my point of view being that if they were not brought up that way, I wouldn't have been either. Needless to say, I always lost.

If I hadn't behaved according to their wishes, they certainly would have felt some inadequacy in relation to their own peers socially (mostly Greek people), besides being angry with me.

I know for a fact that those of Greek origin with whom I matured tended to be more secluded than I.

There were numerous instances when after becoming totally disgusted I would mutter to myself, "Why do I have to be Greek." This statement of my hostility toward my ethnic roots had to be overcome to enable me to mature.

Religion also played an important part in my marginality. Being of the Eastern Orthodox faith, I've often felt myself being classified as a "not quite" (i.e., not quite a Catholic, Protestant, or Jew). This attitude created many unrealistic thoughts about me; principally that I was an atheist, the idea stemming from the fact that Orthodoxy is not an exceptionally well-recognized religion in the United States.

I uninquisitively and fervently followed the doctrines of my church for about 16 years. However, as I matured, troublesome ideas pervaded my basic religious thoughts. "Am I really in the right religion? Is Orthodoxy the correct way to worship God?" And, most important, "How do I really find out?"

Unfortunately, I never went directly to my parents for an answer. At this age I'm afraid I saw their punitive aspects more clearly than their sympathetic ones. "Parents were seen as the providers of one's physical needs and as capricious arbiters of punishment." My reasoning was really unwarranted because I had never, to my recollection, been physically punished—maybe it was this first physical abuse which I unrealistically feared.

Regardless, I regularly attended church, but without my parents. Both were somehow legitimately busy on that day (my father with business and my mother in preparing a big Sunday meal—a Greek custom). As I think back, I remember the envy within me at seeing families go to and from church. The trite saying "the family that prays together, stays together," had real meaning for me.

I think this is a prime factor in my marginality: that although I tried to "be like the other kids" in every possible way—the lack, on the surface, of emotional family ties contributed to my anxiety and prevented me from doing so.

The parent-child relationship of my own experience in religion was a "Do as I say not as I do" attitude. If it had been on a "Do it with me" level, then I would have, with very little anxiety, accepted the purpose and validity of churchgoing.

Perhaps this area of social activity best exemplifies my marginality. Earlier, I stated that emotionally—on the surface—my family ties were poor. This was true but largely unavoidable because both my parents were products of their one environment, whereas I was competing in two. Moreover, they didn't have to contend with two specific sets of values as I did. My father, the epitome of the strong-silent type, worked very hard all of his life. Often he was so tired that after dinner he would just fall asleep. My mother, proper and meticulous in her every quality, was strongly attached to her own parents in childhood and later life. Unconsciously, I believe, she attempted to control me in like manner.

Although there was a definite paucity of showable affection, my parents for 18 years, in the way they assumed to be correct, provided for my welfare and betterment. I always respected and loved them, despite my actions. However, I don't believe they quite understood my situation. I was largely denied the right to explore, feel, or think on my own, as my peers did. Often I was denied permission to go to the show with the guys or spend a night at a friend's house because I never knew "what they were like." I was frequently asked, "Why do you have to? Don't we let you play ball all the time? Besides, you're never home." The first "why" question utterly astounded me when trying to explain that I wanted to be like the other kids, but I could never find the words to express it that way. If I did find a legitimate answer, their retaliation was that I'd do as they said and not as the other kids did. Eventually this attitude, coupled with marginal feelings, drove me beyond their restrictions—this was my problem from a social standpoint.

If a person "is marginal in his family (feels 'left out' emotionally, physically or psychologically), we expect originality to emerge." In my case this originality was trying to do and be like my peers in as many ways as possible. It was largely impossible for me to integrate or express tendencies that were unapproved of by them.

In continuation of this, in high school my "heterosexual life" began in a clandestine manner. I wanted to be like the group, more so than ever now because I was older and had been restricted (in my own thinking) all too long. I began to date and attend dances, often using ridiculous excuses, because my parents thought I was too young for that sort of thing. In a sense, I wanted to "keep up with the Joneses." Hostility arose between my parents and myself, as they knew I hadn't been truthful with them. A deep sense of guilt was constantly about me because I knew my actions were contrary to their wishes.

I can still remember thinking, "How can they deny me these good times which certainly won't harm me?" My uneducated guess as a youth, that I was being brought up strictly only because they had been (a point which they always argued), bore some truth. I have found that parents often unconsciously deny their offspring the opportunities to enjoy the good times which they themselves have missed.

WALLS COME TUMBLING

Shattering of a "nice, meaningful world"

I HAVE LEARNED from historians that there are many religions and all of them claim to be right yet have done wrong; that there were many wars and much politics but little concern for right and wrong; that the story of history is one sentence long— Man is born, he suffers, he dies!

I have learned from political scientists that good old democracy is not accepted as right all over; that, in fact, it has an ideological enemy called communism. I have learned from Marx that capitalists are exploiting me and religion is an opium for the masses.

I have learned from anthropologists that man lives in a civilized jungle where survival of the fittest still rules; that man is a suborder of primates known as homosapiens; that among his cousins are Limers, Tasiers, monkeys, and apes; that my ancestors were Australopithecinae or man-apes from South Africa; that, in short, man is an animal who doesn't like to admit it. I have learned from anthropologists that there are many societies.

I have learned from astronomers and geologists that the earth is an insignificant hunk of metal and rock, in one of a billion insignificant solar systems; that it whirls around in space at a phenomenal speed for a phenomenal distance; and that it is precariously balanced by conflicting forces of gravity—a magical substance we cannot see.

I have learned from psychologists that I am not a truly rational being; that I am a spiritual battlefield between the "id," the "ego," and the "super ego"; that I pass through various stages of development, as a product passes through a conveyor belt in a factory; that I was born a savage baby—a bundle of drives—and that cultures and environment have so wonderfully civilized me; as it civilized Hitler, Mussolini, Stalin, Chou En Lei, Machiavelli, and Marx.

51

I have been told that I long to die and return to the womb; that outwardly I'm an adult but inwardly I'm still a child; that I project, that I rationalize, and that I repress; yes, particularly that I repress. I have been told that whether I'm distrustful, shameful, doubtful, or feel guilty; that whether I'm impulsive, aggressive, or introverted, withdrawn, meek is dependent on the way I was weaned and toilet trained. I have learned that I'm motivated by a pleasure principle and that I'm sexually frustrated but don't know it, or at least don't dare to realize it. Finally, that I'm in a period termed adolescence or young adulthood, or, as Freud called it—the genital stage; that outside of gaining pleasure derived from mature sexual relations with the opposite sex—which I'm not allowed to have, I am primarily concerned with those silly questions: What is it all about? Who am I? Where am I going and why? In short, I have learned that I am nothing better than a modified "id," and a confused one at that!

Let me relate to you my experience since entering college. I am a psychology major and I plan on doing social work— whatever that might be. When I think back, I was guided toward this direction by my religion and the contact I had with an emotionally disturbed friend. I was a good Catholic, if there is such a thing, and I came to school to carry out the mission God had sent me on. The point is, I came to school with ideals and my life had meaning. I felt secure in my society, in my family, in my religion, with my God. I was confident that the world was all right. It was all right because it had meaning, because it was humane, because it was divinely created.

It took twelve years for me to obtain that all-important high school diploma—which seems so insignificant now. During this process I was taught, although some say indoctrinated, that democracy was good and communism was bad; that this country was right, morally and socially, and that "that" country was wrong. I felt that patriotism, loyalty, and faith in God were genuine, good, and widespread. I knew my religion was right and that "theirs" was misguided. The Bible was infallible and Christianity was the answer to the problems of the world. I thought this was general knowledge and all intelligent people knew it.

Yes, I came to college, and lo and behold, my nice meaningful world was shattered—for this I was bitter, frustrated, and
depressed. For the first time I felt that terrible void. And the
questions came flowing out. What am I doing here? Where am
I going? Why? What does it all mean? It seemed ironic that I
was paying to become confused and frustrated.

In relating this to myself, and in view of the fact that my old
world is irretrievably lost, I, as many college students, am trying
to adjust and find a new perspective in my life. During the past
two years knowing where I'm going and why or, in short, what
is the meaning of my life, has been most important.

I realize I'm going through a normal stage and that I will
adjust to it. The thing that concerns me is how I will adjust. A
person could find meaning in his life by his achievement or accomplishment. But is accomplishment enough motivation in
itself? If a person, for example, drilled little holes in little parts
that go into other parts and other parts and other parts that
make up a final part or product, and never know the purpose
of his work except to make money, he cannot, in my opinion,
find meaning in his work. This person must find meaning else-
where; someone he loves, a religion, some other goal—possibly
even suffering.

I might find some meaning in my life by the career I pursue.
Of course, this depends on the individual; some people may find
meaning in a career, while others may not. The point I'm trying
to make, with difficulty, is that my life's work may be enough to
supplement and override the loss of my "shattered world." It's
interesting to note that I find my greatest doubts, insecurities,
and concerns while I'm in school. It may be because I'm forced
to think more about myself, and it could possibly be because
I'm not realizing my career. This may be difficult to understand
because it's difficult to explain.

I first noticed differences in my attitudes when I changed
from school to work. In school I get tied up with day-to-day
things and I think in terms of tests, papers, and grades. I tend
to lose perspective of my career plans. I realize that school is a
preparation for my career but it is not my career. This creates
a sort of void or restlessness. It's like planning to paint your

car. You're anxious to paint it, but you must put this off until you prepare the body.

Many college students have difficulty holding a belief in God. This is, I believe, why many have difficulty finding a meaning in their lives. In the past I've asked many of my college friends what religion they were. Some were agnostic, some atheist, some skeptical, and unconcerned, and some just not sure. It's easy to understand why they have those doubts because I've felt the same doubts. However, this is not the place to go philosophical or theological. I hold God as a value and hope I will continue to do so. The point here is that many people can not find meaning in God. This often leads to free love with the accent completely on sex, rebellion in forms of delinquency and nonconformity, to a state of no achievement. I'm not against rebellion and nonconformity and, to a small degree, free love when it's goal-oriented, but to rebel and not conform as a reaction to giving up is wasteful. I want to stress here that in no way am I saying that everyone should find meaning in the value of God, but that everyone should find meaning! Everyone has a different meaning, although many people do find meaning through God.

I don't suffer in school, although at times I pretend I do, yet I do sacrifice. This sacrifice has a purpose—a meaning important only to myself—and when I have this purpose clearly in mind the sacrifice "ceases to be a sacrifice in some way." It takes on meaning! It should and can be this way in life. We are bound to suffer and to be unhappy; but if our attitude toward suffering is healthy, we will find a meaning in suffering.

In concluding, I would like to say that if I thought that all my suffering in school, at work, at home, or wherever I may be, had no goal, had no purpose, had no meaning; if I thought that I was nothing but a chemical reaction, a blob of protoplasm, a bunch of molecules, a modified *id;* if I thought I was born only to suffer and die, then I would *give up.* Although I can give no simple, logical meaning nor draw any new conclusion nor give any scientific or logical ways of defining my concept of meaning, I feel that one exists. It may be different to me than to you or others. It may change from time to time. I might never realize the meaning and only feel there is one.

FOUR REASONS

Troubles of an early maturing male

I BELIEVE THAT I live a unique life as, I assume, everyone does. But I believe I can substantiate my claims with the forceful statement that I have experienced all that there is to experience in life except marriage and my own death. Seriously, I believe in this statement; I may be limited in a lot of areas, but nevertheless I have the minimum basic experiences to validate my statement.

First, let me jump immediately to my early adolescent period around the age of 11 or 12 and pick out one instance in my life.

As I remember it, at this early date, I never indulged in masturbation. My first wanderings and experiments in any sexual behavior took what I'd call an abnormal course. I will now state this abnormal sexual experience and then try to explain (to the best of my ability) why I ever behaved this way.

That particular first recognition and experience in sexual activity took place shortly after I had undergone all physical changes accompanying puberty and the transition to adolescence. This first experience consisted of my trying to force my bowel movement not to come out by pushing it back with my hand. And in connection with this I also used to insert into my anal opening articles that were in all cases (thank God) slender and long in shape.

To say these (more than once) early experiments were disturbing is an understatement. Even today I wonder what pleasure I got out of this, or whether I was completely nuts, or whether there is an answer to why I indulged in such behavior. Therefore, I believe it is necessary to look at some of the possible causes which resulted in that behavior. Some possible reasons are listed below:

1. I may have been definitely abnormal.
2. It may have some reference to my toilet training days.

3. It may have been the result of inadequate knowledge of proper sex outlets and an ignorance in sex education as a whole.
4. Or it may have been the result of a combination of factors involving sex-role identity, parent-child relations, religion, and anxiety feelings.

The first reason I definitely throw out. And mainly because I only indulged in this type of behavior for a period of two months. Also, after this brief period of two months, I returned to normal activity (which for me could only consist of sports), and put all sexual activity aside for the time being. I assume this sexually inactive period was being normal (after my first experiences, it is a wonder I *ever* tried again).

The second reason or cause (toilet training) may have some bearing on the case, but I have no way of finding out how I was toilet trained. And if there is some connection between my behavior and toilet training, I can't see it at all too clearly. I was a bedwetter until I was 10 years old, but this seems to stem from other sources than toilet training (most likely my avid anxiety and aggression problems). One interesting idea I have formulated is that having come to adolescence, my already vivid rebellious attitudes were augmented greatly. And perhaps I reverted to my toilet training days where perhaps I had resisted authority not only by refusing to toilet train properly but more than likely by messing my pants as well. If that had been the case, then it seems to me that this idea in itself cannot be true. Because in my life now I am not exquisitely neat nor am I the opposite—a complete slob. This whole toilet training idea puzzles me greatly, and I can't figure it out.

The third reason is a little more sensible. My parents had never given me any insight in regard to sexual matters, nor even the basic facts. They had not prepared me for the sudden and demanding feelings I experienced in my early adolescence. I have since also discovered that none of my brothers and sisters ever received any sex education either.

I obtained most of my sex education via my male friends, and often with not a little embarrassment. One particular instance is very clear in my mind. It occurred at a place where all of the "guys" were having a bull session around the campfire. The main topic of conversation was masturbation. This occurred about a year and a half after the bowel movement episodes. I got into the conversation by asking quite timidly what this was. The guys told me with a dazed look. I was 13½ at this time and I was well developed for my age. I was a so-called early maturer. I did extremely well in sports and I was always fighting and winning. I was at this time the ring leader for my age group, and they were shocked that I would be the one to ask such a question. In reply to their comment on what it was, I immediately replied, "Oh, so that's what it is!" and I continued by saying, "Sure." But in actuality, I had never had an orgasm and was next to ignorant on the whole subject.

What a blow my ego took. Here I was the toughest kid in my group and half the punks I had clobbered could masturbate and I couldn't. This *was* an embarrassing moment in my "sex education by buddies," but more so, it shows how really inadequate my whole knowledge of sex was. What made it seem even worse was the fact that I didn't start masturbating until I was 14 years old. A funny sidelight is the fact that after that discussion I would think of the dirtiest, most perverted daydreams, but I'd be darned if anything would happen.

It was a few months after that I had my first orgasm. It was through nocturnal emission and was accompanied by the usual erotic dream. However, when this occurred, I had already heard the term "wet dream," and I was not particularly affected, except that I loved it. It was shortly after this first orgasm that I started masturbating. Remember, for quite a while I had been trying my best to think up the most erotic daydreams in an effort to produce that white sticky stuff. Well, on this particular occasion, I had been reading *Peyton Place* when all of a sudden it dawned on me that instead of imposing my will on my penis, I should impose my hand. Needless to say, I had some catching up to do and I proceeded with great vigor. From this point on, I only had relatively minor difficulties with heterosexual relationships, mainly guilt when I first indulged.

More than being a humorous narrative, the instances I have described show to what a large degree I had needed the proper sex education. I might also add a peculiar fact concerning this period and that was that I never once directed any questions on sex matters to either of my parents. What bearing does this seemingly insignificant fact have on the case we are studying? And this brings me to the fourth item on my list of reasons— the combination of factors.

In connection with the combination of factors, I would like to start with sex-role identification and proceed from there. But before I do another thing, I had better reveal some more of my private life and childhood.

Both my father and mother were strict, my father more so. I would say that they were more than normally strict.

My father worked during the day, and being as strict as my parents were, we were all in bed at seven o'clock sharp each evening. Consequently, there was not much time to be spent with my father. I had an older brother who couldn't be bothered with his little brother. When I was born it was at a time when my nearest siblings were all girls, and if I was not playing with them at any time, I was more than likely being babied by one of them. And of course my mother was always present for me.

So we see early in my life where I may have had some problem identifying with the correct sex model. And although most arrows point in the direction that I would develop a very feminine sex role—I didn't! I believe that I don't have many, if any, feminine characteristics. I matured physically very early in adolescence. I was very aggressive, to the point that I was recommended for psychiatric care for getting into so many fights. I excelled in all areas considered masculine; I even developed fairly well-rounded heterosexual relationships. Then how did I turn out so "masculine" if my childhood was so dominated by "femininity"? My answer is that in being exposed to such an overdose of feminine sex-role models and feminine characteristics, I rebelled against them all. I asserted my masculinity even more forcefully and determinedly than I would have under normal conditions.

I believe that, untrained as I am, I really can't make a correct hypothesis, although this matter is one which I would thoroughly enjoy understanding.

I would say that parent-child relations, anxiety feelings, and excessive aggressive attitudes are all very closely related to each other and to the subject at hand.

My father died when I was 15 years old, and the relation of my aggressive behavior and anxiety feelings to this happening seems enormous, because it was shortly after my father died that I had the most trouble controlling them both. However, when I think back and take a better look at my childhood, I can see where the most pertinent reasons for overaggressiveness and anxiety had their origins much earlier than my father's death. When my father was alive I had a fair parent-child relationship with him, though it left much to be desired.

As I have previously mentioned, my father was always working. He had to spread his fatherly love out quite thin. Whenever he could, my father tried his best to spend as much time with me as he could. But more often than not, my father was mainly the authoritative hand of punishment. I did fear my father, of that there is no doubt. And it seemed that I never could please him. It was later on that I found out that, to the contrary, my father was always quite proud of me. He was so overwhelmed with worries and providing us with a roof over our heads that he simply could not express or show openly any feelings of pride that he felt for me. But regardless, the negation of feelings caused me to be alienated from my father and to fear him. Since I grew up with the feelings that I was never pleasing my father, I was even more motivated to do well in everything I tried.

Fear of my father may have caused me to keep my curiosity concerning sex well contained within myself and directed away from him. Well, if I could not talk to my father and if I had a wonderful mother-child relationship, then why didn't I approach my mother? Well, I obviously didn't and for two different reasons. The first concerns independence and the second concerns religion.

Having many children, neither of my parents could afford to baby us or be overprotective with any of us. In my case, even though my parents were strict, I was *very* independent. I would usually go off by myself each day (if I could ever get rid of my sisters) and be seen only at mealtimes, and, for the most part, I got a good smack for being late. This independence of mine was really quite strong. Even with this good relationship with my mother, I could never bring myself to become dependent on and confide in her. Even the time when I caught my penis in my zipper I had to half bleed to death before I'd tell either of my parents what happened.

In studying further this situation where I was always dependent on no one but myself and wouldn't even confide in my mother, I can see a correlation in the fact that there may have been and actually was a lack of nurturance in my infant and childhood days. When I examine my life then and now, I must admit I don't trust a blessed soul nor ever did. I might add in connection with this that I have always hated the world.

I'd give special consideration to this idea of a lack of nurturance and also to a previously expressed idea, the one of alienation from my father. It is these two concepts that I believe are the main bases for my excessive aggressiveness and often acute anxiety. It would be interesting to explore these two in depth, but suffice it to say, I haven't changed much at all and am still very aggressive, bitter, and anxious, to say the least. Besides, I want to return to the problem at hand—what were the possible causes for that peculiar behavior of my very early adolescence.

All of the issues that I am expounding—alienation, lack of nurturance, religion, and relative independence—are pertinent to the "case" in that they all acted in unison to keep me from confiding in or seeking answers from either my mother or my father in regard to the many questions I wanted to ask about sex.

I mentioned religion in connection with this discussion because I do feel that it plays a part. I am Catholic, and, in the Catholic religion, the confirmation ceremony occurs when the child is in the seventh or eighth grade and usually coincides roughly with the onset of puberty and the new feelings of sexuality accompanying it. Before you do get confirmed, there is an extensive preparation period which is supposed to rejuvenate any lag in your religious potential. Confirmation itself means that you have become a "soldier in the army of God." Despite my aggressiveness, my earlier adolescent and preadolescent days were fairly religious ones. And, with confirmation coming when it did, this bolstered all of my religious feeling. And during or just prior to this massive dose of religion the behavior we have been discussing took place. I am not saying that religiousness is the cause of this behavior, but I do think that this brief period of high religiousness, at that particular time, was one of the contributing factors to why I never confided in or consulted anyone on sex.

My deep feelings on religion also made me feel quite guilty over this behavior and later on in my first explorations of heterosexual experiences. I mentioned earlier how I had loved my first orgasm (via nocturnal emission). Well, in that case I did, and not too many guilt feelings accompanied this at all. I had heard of wet dreams and I had also heard that they weren't considered a sin, but rather as nature taking its own course. Later, though, when I started masturbating, the feelings of guilt were something to cope with. And, to this day, I'd love to thrash the pious person who said sex isn't healthy and is a sin except when you are married. The troubled hours I used to spend mooning over imminent damnation were almost unbearable.

A LOST FEELING

Longing for a real father

BEING A FATHERLESS CHILD, I would like to mention some of my own childhood feelings as I best remember. I am sometimes amazed at the seeming vividness with which I recall these.

My father was killed in World War II when I was an infant. In early childhood, realizing what a "daddy" was and that I did not have one, I developed a "lost" feeling. I would frequently lose myself in daydreams, trying to find his image, and had many dreams of him at night. I sought someone I could call "Daddy"—the name had a special magic, a joyous connotation. My mother and I made frequent visits to one particular family —my aunt, uncle, and cousins. To this day I remember sitting on my uncle's knee, feeling the roughness of his beard, and asking, "Can I call you daddy?" I don't recall his answer, but I do know that I never did use the name to him. He was "Uncle Bennett" and nothing could change this. The name "daddy," to me, could only mean someone I would never know.

I was often told how wonderful he was—how I would have loved him and how he would have cherished me. This often made me feel sad, and I would cry—as I still sometimes do today. But even as a very young child I knew that I could be proud of him because he died for his country.

Having a male teacher for the first time pleased most of the children, but it delighted me beyond words. I couldn't understand my friends' lack of outward enthusiasm. Although I was eager to receive attention and approval from the teacher, I was rather quiet in class. I don't recall any particular incident, but I do know that I did well in my work, that this was the only grade through school in which I had perfect attendance.

I clearly remember an incident with my mother at home, that was repeated a number of times. My mother has two framed pictures of my father. One, in which he wears dress clothes, is very small and is in black and white. The other, in which he wears his uniform, is large and in color. The large one was kept in the dresser drawer, the smaller one on top. My mother insisted that the smaller picture was better, for it looked more like him—she did not care for the larger one. I was forever taking out the larger picture and putting it on my desk. I thought it was beautiful. I often hesitated to ask about my father, thinking it would make my mother sad, so I would look endlessly at the pictures. Sometimes she did speak of him, and I loved to listen. Whenever she mentioned anything I did "just like your father" I tried to do it whenever the chance arose, knowing it made her happy.

Through high school, the feeling of pride, which began so many years before, continued to grow stronger. Each year every senior student in the history and government classes would write an essay on the meaning of Memorial Day. Five or six of these were chosen to be read at a Memorial Day assembly. I think my essay summed up my feelings for my "daddy." As I read it at the assembly, I was not seeking sympathy, I was not angry at the world for war—I was proud.

I have made an image and have clung to it as a "substitute father" for many years, and will probably continue to do so forever. But as I grow older, my main concern is not that of a father for myself. It is the hope that my children will have a father when a father is most needed—throughout childhood.

TO SHED A SHELL

Struggling with inferiority feelings

THERE ARE PHYSICAL GROWTH FACTORS during middle childhood. By the time the average male is twelve, he is 60 inches tall and weighs between 95 and 100 pounds. When I was twelve, I was about 56 inches tall and weighed about 65 pounds. I guess I could be called a "late maturer." Usually a late-maturing male doesn't do well socially or athletically, so he puts all his spare time on his studies to advance academically, but in my case it wasn't so. As a matter of fact, I got average to poor marks throughout junior and senior high school. I wouldn't say that I wouldn't have done well athletically, but I didn't get a chance to prove myself because of my size. I didn't even make the Little League baseball teams because of physical and social reasons. I was too small and I was much too shy. I probably was so shy because of my size, and let too many people dominate me. Some of the boys who tried out were not as good as I was, but they made the teams.

Influence of the family affects the individual in his middle childhood years. In my case, I was the youngest. Besides my mother and father, I had three older brothers and an older sister, who is also the oldest in the family. Between each child, there is about four years, and I grew up in a neighborhood where there were no other children of my age and my brother closest to me in age was too old to play with because he was always that much more mature. I was always ordered around by my older brothers and sister, but I had no one younger than myself to order around. I believe I was about six years old before another boy of my age moved into the neighborhood. By this time, it was time to go to school anyway. In school I had a hard time getting adjusted, mainly because I was too shy. I would daydream a lot and the teacher would yell at me. I soon became terrified of teachers. I went to an old, small school. It was so small that we had two grades in each room. The teacher would alternate hours of instruction with each.

I think that when I went to school a great change came over me, mainly because I got to know certain peer groups. I became acquainted with children my own age, including girls, who terrified me, partly because they were all bigger than I.

As I passed into the adolescent period, I had some of the old problems, and found some new ones. I was still the smallest boy in school. My friends were starting to excel in sports such as football and basketball. I was too light for football and too short for basketball. I needed something to prove my masculinity. Somewhere along the line, I found out that I could run fast. As a matter of fact, I was one of the fastest runners in high school. This solved one problem, but there were still others. The other boys were interested in girls now and were even dating. My parents reminded me constantly to stay away from girls until I finished school. I became very bashful when it came to talking to a girl. Stay away from them I did. I didn't have one date throughout high school. In fact, I was about the only boy who didn't go to the senior prom.

As I entered my sophomore year in high school, I was the same person I had been two or three years before. The only thing I had going for me was the fact that I was a good runner and an asset to the track team. But then I got pneumonia and had to give up all forms of recreation for a year. This sickness brought me down to 73 pounds. My doctor suggested that I lift weights to build myself up. Within two years I had put on about 50 pounds and added about eight inches in height. When my physical development advanced, so did my social development. You might say that I "came out of my shell" somewhat. I began to develop a personality and didn't find much trouble talking.

My parents may be the "old-fashioned" type, but there are some advantages that I received. For example, I don't smoke and am one of the few persons my age that doesn't. Also, I have stayed out of trouble, which is not the case with a lot of the "early maturing" males. This is because they received more freedom when they were younger.

I am now 19 years of age, but I still have a few problems. Actually, I'm afraid to be 19 because I'm not mentally or socially equipped to be that age. Maybe I am. In fact, my biggest problem is the fact that I have a very bad inferiority complex, which has prevented me from being myself many times. My father has always gotten me jobs for the summer when I needed them. Whenever I went for an interview for a job or at school, he went along with me. I was never given a chance to be independent of my overprotective parents. Just in the past year or two have I begun to be somewhat independent.

I do not go out on too many dates, although I know and get along with a great many girls. Something that worries me is the fact that I have three brothers married and they went steady with their girlfriends for about five years. This puts me about two years behind schedule according to them.

Possibly my problems stem from the fact that I never developed a strong "ego identity" or self-concept in my adolescence. A number of psychologists and psychiatrists have pointed out that the adolescent in our culture is vitally concerned with assessing his liabilities and assets, trying on various roles to see which fit him the most comfortably. An adolescent, during this period, chooses long-term goals which will influence the course of his behavior for the rest of his life. Only a couple of years ago I finally decided what I wanted to be. Maybe I chose to be an educator because I want to give boys the chances I never had. Although I consider myself very skillful now in sports and acquire these skills very easily, these skills came to me late in my adolescence.

I have my certain goals in life all planned and am no longer afraid to go after them. Besides raising my own family, I would like to be a very successful teacher. The most important thing to me is that every boy gets a chance to prove himself, not only the ones with natural talent, but also the ones who have much room for improvement. There is nothing I hate more than a lazy student. I would like to be in a good education program in the school where I may work and catch problems while the kids are still young enough to do something about it; to develop them in mind, body, and spirit, and to make gentlemen of them.

CLOSE THE WINDOWS

"Caught up" in unrealistic attitudes

I CANNOT CONCEIVE HOW a society so involved in the ideals of freedom of action and choice, so dedicated to the actions of making life more comfortable for the underprivileged peoples of the world, can adopt for its own members a cultural foundation so incongruous and conflicting. I have often wondered why citizens would allow them to remain functional for as long as they have. Perhaps there is some correlation between the two trains of thought. To me, this correlation is of little importance as compared to the desire to reconstruct our values. Little, in my opinion, has actually been done. But this is not the crux of my discussion, so I shall let it lie dormant for a while. After all, if we've let it go for so many years, a few minutes should not make a big difference.

As I recollect, the first time I was made aware of the strictness of our culture was when, at the age of eleven, my mother and I had a detailed discussion of the facts of life. My sister, who was also included in the conversation, was about ten years old. Although I had enquired as to where babies came from earlier (about age seven), the response then was not as enlightening.

The thing that remains the most poignant in my mind is not so much the information discussed (which I feel is seldom retained), as the manner in which we were informed. We had been told earlier in the day that my mother wanted us to come in from playing at 3:00 P.M. When we went into the living room, my mother told us to close the windows. This seemed strange seeing as how the weather was so warm. Yet she insisted. I know now that she didn't deem it wise to have the kids outside overhear the extent of the conversation. However, after hearing what she had to say, I felt that there was something secretive or even wrong with sex. At this point, it might be surmised by the reader that my mother's actions were but an individual example, not actually applicable as a manifestation of how our culture plays down the role of sex in our lives. I doubt this is the case. My mother is a woman whose ideas about sex are, in my opinion, very liberal. I feel that it is for the very reason that society pressures us to act in certain ways, contrary oftentimes to the manner in which we wish to act, that my mother was "forced" to act the way she did.

It has been stated by many psychologists that our culture is a conflict-arousing one. This can be seen in the culture's shifting of requirements for social acceptability in regard to relations with opposite sex peers. I remember that when I was about 10 or 11 years old, I had very little to do with girls. I was busy playing war or construction, or any game which by its nature prevented girls from taking part. My friends and I used to spend some time ridiculing them or playing tricks on them. Some of them were quite clever. In one, for instance, we used to have one of the boys run up to a group of girls playing with their "sissy" dolls and inform them that if they left everything where it was and hurried over to a certain place (where they couldn't see their doll carriages), they would be able to see a real live dead cat. After some coaxing, they would usually leave. At this time, the rest of us would surreptitiously either hide their dolls or mess them up. We had a ball. We usually got away with it when the girls told the parents. We'd get a little scolding every now and then; but that was all. Boys our age were supposed to act like that. We were just normal kids growing up.

Then it seemed like everything changed. All of a sudden, a couple of the guys started paying quite a bit of attention to these girls; too much attention, as far as we were concerned. It was a while before the rest of us came around to the same line of thinking. During that time, we never quite got away with playing the same old tricks or making fun of the girls. All of a sudden, the parents were on the girls' side. They wanted us to treat them nicely, like little ladies.

During this time, there were a lot of conflicting ideas about our relations with girls. We'd even have to dress up and go to their birthday parties, treat them politely, and so forth. Our pride was shattered. We were degraded. Until we all changed our ideas about girls, we were under quite a bit of pressure. Our interest in girls was brought about by the physiology of our bodies. Yet I can't help but think that, in part, it was also brought about by outside pressure.

Most of the conflict was brought about by our cultural dogmas. Was it, or is it necessary? Is there a better way to go through this period?

When I was about fourteen or so, I cannot be too precise about it, I went to parties with girls, enjoyed their company, liked to be thought of highly and admired for my masculinity by them. There was little actual tension or conflict that I am aware of in regard to the relationships, except the anxiety or nervousness in doing the right thing at the right time in their presence. As far as the sexual aspect is concerned, there was a progressive quality to the extent of holding hands or later even a good-night kiss.

It wasn't until I was about sixteen that the more advanced stages of sexual behavior came to light. At parties, I remember having the girl sitting on my lap with nothing other than kissing as the main order of the day. It was in progression from this that the petting came into being. I'm not saying that prior to this time there had been no petting or bodily contact. At earlier times, it was for curiosity or exploration. During the latter time period, it was done more for purely sexual gratification than anything else.

During this time, there was much information tossed into my face concerning the malignancy and immorality of sex. To my surprise, it came not so much from my parents as it did from outside sources. In school, my class (9th grade) got a lecture on how we should conduct ourselves at the annual spring dance. We had to force back the laughter, let alone the smiles. According to the teacher, we were hardly allowed to hold hands when we danced. We received this type of information from other public school teachers, as well. Once, our minister and his wife held separate meetings with the girls and boys of our youth group, the minister speaking to the boys, and his wife to the girls. Both adults were sincere in telling us of the evils of petting and necking. Most of the boys thought the whole talk was childish, including myself. I would say that although the listening body was a mixed age group (14 to 19), a good majority had already experienced much of what was being tabooed. However, I recollect taking notice of a few boys who were prime targets for such a discussion.

I don't want it to appear that I'm in favor of letting sex run wild, but I do feel that such discussions and lectures that are handed down by adults, and merely reflect the cultural pressures, are oftentimes quite harmful in forming adverse lines of reasoning in the younger child's mind in regard to sex. A possible example of this may be that at the end of our lectures, when we were invited to the rectory for refreshments, there was a strict line of segregation voluntarily set up by some of the girls and boys. Later on in the evening, this segregation was broken. Was it just a passing phase or did it leave, at least in some, a serious detriment in sexual terms of reasoning?

From this stage of adolescence until marriage, there appear a number of conflicting ideas and questions concerning the sexual relationships between opposite sex peers. These problems manifest themselves to a higher degree in the individual whose relationship with the opposite sex is limited to one girl. It is at this time that the specific information of functional organs, reproduction and the like, is replaced (though never forgotten) with more intense problems. Questions such as "What is love?" "Is masturbation harmful in curbing sexual gratification?" "Is it right or wrong to have intercourse before marriage?" "Is petting right or wrong?" It seems to me that it is important to know how to use sex and what its limits are rather than to know that women are capable of supplying eggs which are known as ova.

Our culture seems adverse to all the physiological pressures exerted on the adolescent. This I can safely state, due to my own personal relations with the girl I intend to marry, and due to the many discussions I have had with people in the same situation. That there is a very definite conflict in our culture may be seen in the formation of a corresponding set of rules and philosophy by some adolescents. An example of what I mean is the statement which, by the way, is almost unanimously accepted, that "I don't care who the people are. If they've been going steady for over a year, they've had intercourse." This statement applies to people in the later adolescent stage, and although it has been noted that upper middle class adolescents are less likely to experience intercourse before marriage than those of a lower class, I have found this statement to be representative of a great many upper class people. You must realize that these ideas are not the result of documented experiments. However, I don't feel that they should be disregarded for this reason.

I should like to devote the next few paragraphs to a discussion of adolescents going steady—if I may be allowed to use a cliché—and those in the later adolescent/early adult status. I realize that many people never leave adolescence, but I do not feel it necessary to be that technical in word choice at this time.

It is generally felt, from the adolescent's point of view, that people who are going steady experience several added conflicts, usually more anxiety-arousing, than "single" individuals. The most intense of these problems is that of deciding whether or not premarital sexual relations are right or wrong, and what actions are to be taken in regard to either reconciliation. Usually, either one of the two produces anxiety-arousing situations. I think most people will agree that deciding whether or not to have premarital sexual relations is in itself a main conflicting area for the adolescent, let alone planning one's actions accordingly.

Let us suppose that certain decisions have been reached on this question. Now let us see how, if at all, the answer will produce anxiety and conflict, and compare them later.

If the male has decided that it is not immoral to have intercourse, he has probably gone against the admonitions and hope of his parents, as well as the cultural mores. There is a great deal of anxiety and tension involved. Once he has acted accordingly, he might resign himself to the fact that there is a chance that the girl may become pregnant. By this time, he may or may not have experienced the intensely conflicting and anxiety-arousing experience of fearing that his girl *might* be pregnant. He now plans on seeing that he and his girl friend do not indulge again (until marriage, of course). There is anxiety in trying to give up the pleasure he has enjoyed and taking into consideration the feelings of the girl.

But what if the male has decided that premarital sexual relations are immoral? There still remains the anxiety of having to consider a line of action contrary to the laws set by his parents and society. There is also the conflict over how to inhibit his desires and those of the girl, if he has any feelings whatsoever. Will masturbation successfully curb the desire? Is it harmful? These questions and their answers are sure to produce psychological disturbances.

In regard to the degree to which these choices vary as anxiety-arousing situations, I doubt that there can be an accurate comparison because of the great number of differences in each of us.

In this "undocumented" discussion, I hope it can be seen that the most impressive fact formulated is that much of the anxiety and psychological disturbances are a product of the strict and contrary laws, customs, doctrines, and mores of our culture. A great deal of this tension could be avoided were it not for the narrow-minded, puritanical cultural traits that have endured for so long a time. If it were possible for the individual in our culture to more freely express the *natural* desires and actions attributed to the human animal for thousands of years, I feel that a general change for the better would take place in our society. The problem of morality in accord with sexuality alone plays such an important role in our lives that to twist and contort it to fit our so-called cultural heritage is to twist and contort the development of the inhabitants of the society itself. "Sex" is not a four-letter word. It should not be treated as such.

TONSILS AND THINGS

"Now it seems hilariously funny"

I CAN REMEMBER that I was circumcised at nine years of age. I went to the hospital originally to have my tonsils out. As it turned out, my parents thought I might as well get circumcised at the same time—only one thing, they didn't tell me about it.

Well, I woke up from the anaesthetic and the first thing I felt was a sharp pain in the penis. After a few more such pains, I took off the covers and found that somebody had cut the skin off around my penis. I look back on it now and it seems hilariously funny; but from reports of my parents, they say I was very upset at the thought of not being told it was to be done.

I first thought the absent-minded doctor got me mixed up with another one of his patients, but when my parents came to visit, they informed me that they had decided to have it done. Well, no use crying over what's lost, only I pulled out the little black buds around it. These were the stitches—it's a good thing the skin was relatively healed.

That's about all I can remember in my very young childhood.

I can remember that in my adolescent days, when I was 14 to 15 years old, a girl was trying to tell me and four of my friends about menstruation. She came out with "Girls bleed every month!" I was always sort of slow and I couldn't understand what she was saying. I thought they might get sick or something. Two of my older friends knew and let the other boy and me in on the big deal. I don't know why, but it struck me kind of funny and I laughed like a son of a gun! The girl didn't like that and went home. She's married now and used to go steady with my best friend.

I guess I felt the girls had the worst of the deal and was glad I was a boy.

Also a bunch of the guys would always brag about what they did with what girl and so on. I can remember how the other boys, except me, thought they were "quite the men." The girls seemed to like that kind of boy, too. Then again, some of the girls were a little "soft" anyway.

I was always the quiet, hot-tempered type. I didn't have much to do with any of the girls. I was usually the youngest but one of the biggest guys in the group. A few of the girls liked me but I never cared about it.

I'M LEARNING THOUGH

When idealism becomes a problem

MY PARENTS, BOTH STRICT CATHOLICS, instilled in me a great respect for the church and its teachings. I have lived in a relatively small town all my life.

My father, a life-long resident of the same community, is quite well known. He had to turn down going to college to support his fatherless family. He often expresses his regret for not going to college later on. People in town often call me by my father's name and then excuse themselves.

My mother is the perfect lady. She is very quiet, yet in some ways wears the "pants." This in no way means she is masculine; in fact, she is extremely feminine, but she does handle the money in the family. I should not complain, for if it were not for her, I would not be attending college. She is extremely thrifty and saves every possible cent.

My childhood was normal, yet I must admit that my awareness of sex did not increase at a normal rate. I did not know the genital differences of the sexes until I was about twelve. This unawareness can be attributed to the fact that the circumstances for observing the female body never arose. I didn't masturbate until fifteen and didn't know what many of the sexually connotative words meant until about eighteen. I think that since I was so involved in other activities with the same type of children as myself, I was not overly observant of what went on.

As I said earlier, I was very active as a child. I coasted on snowy cold days for hours and hours, went on bicycle hikes, and played the usual children's games. I was on the Little and Pony League Baseball teams, and played football, baseball, and basketball in my junior high years.

My high school years were productive in a social rather than scholastic sense. My teachers continually complained that I did not work to the best of my ability. While in high school I wrote for the school paper and attended seminars in journalism at colleges and universities as my school representative. I was on the various dance and prom activities, and in the senior play and class day committee. My friends in high school were the football players, cheer leaders, class officers, and other school leaders. The other students ridiculed us behind our backs, calling us "the" clique running the student body. Our moment of triumph came at graduation ceremonies where we reaped the best scholarships. My friends later went on to colleges like Smith, Mt. Holyoke, Amherst, Dartmouth, Notre Dame, the Citadel, and Oberlin. We were not a vicious clique as some felt, just a group of friends who had been buddies for years and naturally continued our friendships throughout high school.

Now, as a third-year college student, I am lost. I get depressed not knowing what's coming next. Following is an examination of my own problems as I see them and what relationship they have with my childhood.

During the past year, my conflicts with my family have increased. While a young adolescent, my main problem was making a name for myself rather than being just "Bill's son"; my problem now consists of seeking greater independence. I want to go out and have a good time, come home when I want to, and be able to decide whether I want to take an apartment in town with some friends of mine. My parents seem to be unwilling to allow me to do the aforementioned things. Their argument is that as long as I'm living under their roof and receiving financial aid from them, I'll continue to do what they say. Whereas some shrink from argument, I fight violently with them. I maintain I'm able to make decisions maturely enough, and they are trying to hold on to me. I use what I learn in school as a substantiation of my argument. Immediately, my father replies, "Just because you're in college, don't think you know more than your mother and me." I think my father resents the fact that he didn't get the college education he wanted, and takes it out on me.

Along with this revolt against my parents for more independence, I have become increasingly lethargic in my church beliefs. For twelve years I was forced to attend religious classes against my will. The church and its principles represent a stumbling block to my free thinking and independence. I want to be free of everything, but this is impossible, for my conscience bothers me for every little infraction I commit, because I have to go to confession. But I feel so hypocritical because I know I'm going to do it again and again, so in the eyes of the church I don't receive absolution. If you don't get absolution and you die, you go to hell . . . . ugh. (If my parents saw this they'd kill me.)

Another problem I've had the past year is the people who ridicule me for my lack of realness in my sexual and personal relationships. People often make remarks about sex and when I don't pick up the meanings, they say I'm anything from stupid, innocent, naive, to too idealistic. As I mentioned before, I never associated with people who talked about sex or used obscene language (notice I differentiate between the two) and naturally I don't know many of these terms. I'm learning, though, although I'm not going out and purposely trying to increase my knowledge of obscenity so I can be a "big" man. I was never really ashamed of this lack of knowledge, and I can learn the proper sexual terms from my mature friends and good textbooks on the subject.

Another point where people think I'm too idealistic is in my conversation. I abhor people who sit down and talk about others. When somebody is "cutting" someone I usually tell them to change the subject and this embarrasses them. People in this situation always jump to their own defense by saying, "Let's be realistic, people talk about me and you so we're not doing anything unusual." I feel that I don't really care what others say about me and I keep three things in mind:

1. I consider myself extremely loyal to my friends—I wouldn't believe anything about them unless they themselves told me and if I had anything to say about them I'd say it directly to them.
2. If I don't know them well I can't say anything and wouldn't believe anything about them until I was able to judge them myself.
3. And if I know and dislike them, I couldn't be bothered with such trivial conversation.

The defense that everybody talks about others is so foolish, but you would be surprised how many "free thinking" (ha) college students use such a defense. Today's college students are such joiners. Examples of these are those students who like folk music because to them those students that appear most "college" like folk music, and those who join the freedom marches but who really don't care what happens to the Negro.

The most alarming of my problems is the complete reversal of the type of friendships I'm making at school. In high school I had seven or eight very close friends; now I have about 68 friends, but none of them as intimate as my high school chums. I don't know whether I did this unconsciously fearing to be labeled as a clique member, but the change is very noticeable. When I remark to a few of my classmates that I don't really have many friends, they usually reply, "What do you mean?" and "You're probably one of the most popular people in the class." But when I think of it, sure, I know and am known by many people, but how many can I really consider the type of friends one can confide his problems in. It is very distressing to me to be able to count them on one finger. This remains my biggest problem: should I sacrifice close friendships for greater popularity. This is a question only I can answer for myself.

THE HORROR SHOW

"Why was I always so jealous?"

THIS IS GOING to be a story of my life. I have never told anyone else a story of my life, so I think it might be interesting for both of us. You have probably heard other life stories before, so maybe this will be old hat to you. I hope not, because I really want to get this off my chest.

I'm not looking for sympathy or anything like that, but sometimes I think that I am, or was, crazy for some of the things that I have done in my life. I don't know, maybe they were all normal, but I never saw anyone else do such nutty things.

First of all, I will say that my home life was always the greatest. I have had everything that I ever wanted, within reason of course. I am the youngest child, so this probably explains why I got almost everything I wanted.

As a youngster I did about the same thing as every other kid. I got in fights, I threatened to run away from home a couple of times that I can remember, the same as any other kid. I disliked girls like all my friends did, but I can remember having a little girl as a friend for quite a while. This girl lived above me in the same house so instead of being enemies, we were friends. We used to play house and all that other rot that kids play.

Well, enough of that stuff. Now I will tell you about my older life. When I get through this paper, I will probably get a big kick out of it, as I know you will.

When I was in the second grade, my parents and I moved from the city to the country. When we were going to move, my father asked me if I wanted to move. I was overjoyed. When he said the country, I thought he meant a place like Texas or something like that. The thing that was in the back of my mind all the time was that there was no school in a place like that, so I would love to live there. Well, come to find out, there was a school. This really had an effect on me. I never wanted to go to school again. It took me a while to get used to the change, but I got by. I always did well in school and got all A's because everything came so easily to me. This probably ruined me for life, because after I got out of grammar school I didn't do as well. As a matter of fact, I don't think I ever got more than one A at a time after those years.

My junior high years were a lot of fun. I can remember laughing more times at the stupidest things. It was great. Everything was a great big bowl of cherries then. No time for girls or anything like that as I was too busy laughing.

I can remember one thing in the eighth grade that had a lot to do with my later life. I met this girl named Jean. She was a great kid and I always used to talk to her during math class. That is where my trouble begins. I guess I kind of liked her because she was the first girl I ever really could talk to like a friend. She must have liked me too, because she told one of my friends she did.

I was too shy or something to ask her out or anything like that, so we were just friends, although I would have liked to have her as my girl friend like some of the other guys had. Nothing ever happened though, not yet.

When I got to the ninth grade, I started playing hockey. This was also a turning point in my life. After this, my whole life was hockey. I never studied or anything like that during hockey season. I loved the game and that was all. I still love hockey, but I don't let it interfere with my life like it used to do. I find quite a difference between high school and college athletics. Not only in the game itself, but in the interest of the students. The kids in college just come to a game to get drunk and find themselves some action for that night.

Well, that has nothing to do with the subject at hand, so I'll forget it for now. Anyway, as I was saying, in the ninth grade I started playing ball. The freshman team was not very good, but I was picked to move up to the varsity for the last game of the season. This was a big deal and quite an honor. We lost the game, but I played a little bit.

I am not trying to brag about myself or make up stories by telling you this. What I am getting at is that being a good athlete made me pretty popular with the girls.

I guess I was pretty good looking, too. That's what I heard, anyway. All right, a couple of girls wanted to go out with me, and I would have liked to take them out. You know something? I could never ask a girl out. I don't know what it was, I just couldn't do it.

If I was at a party or something like that, I could do O.K. with a girl, but I could never ask one to go out with me and me alone.

Well, you can imagine what the girls started to think about me. You know, stuck up, snob, etc. I could almost have given a damn about them or anyone else, for that matter. This is when I took up drinking as a hobby. It was an outlet and sometimes the only thing to do. All of my friends did it too; we used to have a ball. This was only my sophomore year in high school. Oh, I must tell you that I never drank or smoked during hockey season. This is something I am still very proud of. It might not seem like much to you, but that proves how dedicated I was to hockey.

Well, things went on and in my junior year I ran into that girl Jean again. This time things were a little different. I was a little older and I knew a little more about life; you know, I was a little grown up. I took her out a few times but I never really got serious with her. I took her to the junior prom and we went to an all-night party after the prom. Wait till you hear this. I was with her all night and I never kissed her once. Now doesn't that crack you right up? She was really nice stuff, too. I don't know why, but I didn't.

I had been out with other girls that meant nothing to me and had a good time with them, but because this girl really meant a lot to me, I could not touch her. I guess I was just shy or something. What a beaut I am anyway.

Now comes the real horror show of my high school years, my senior year. You wouldn't believe how much one guy could screw up. It was fantastic. But I will say one thing, I never had so much fun in all my life as that year. I would do the same things over again with a few exceptions.

Well, in the end of my junior year I had rolled my car over several times (at once), so I lost my driver's license for an indefinite period. I didn't have a job and I just hung around the house or went to the beach all day. Well, do you know, this girl Jean came down my house and picked me up almost every day? She worked and paid for everything. What a great kid. I still treated her like dirt for some unknown reason.

Her birthday was in April so I decided to get a job and buy a present. I worked for a couple of days and made thirty dollars. This was on a Friday and her birthday was on a Tuesday. You guessed it. Every last cent gone in two days, all spent on beer and eats. Really a good time, but why did I do it? That's why I think I was a nut. Something was wrong. Normal people would not do a thing like that. She still stayed with me though; she was a real sucker—either that or she liked me an awful lot.

In the fall we went back to school and soon it was hockey time again. I was the captain of the team and wanted the team to be the best one yet. We lost almost every game. No one but me and a couple of other kids gave a damn about winning. They just played for the glory and for the girls sitting in the stands.

Now I had a real grudge against the world and everyone in it. Jean was still around and still taking abuse from me. About this time she started to get a little sick of it. I don't blame her now, but then I wanted to kill her. I am very jealous and proud, I guess. Every time I saw her even talking to another guy I would start a big fight. We had more arguments, over such stupid things. I got real mad, too; I even hit her a couple of times.

Once she went out with a kid from out of town. I knew she was going to pull this so I followed them around and beat the devil out of the kid after he brought her home. This started a big fight between my school and the other kid's school. Real great. I almost landed in jail.

I could go on for hours and hours telling you the stupid things I did. Throwing bottles at her house, laying rubber in front of her house, swearing at her real bad; I don't know why I did all these crazy things, but I did.

Well, that about completes the story. Now I can't figure out why it all happened. Why was I always so jealous, so thick-headed, so possessive, etc. I can't really find any reasons.

LET ME COUNT THE WAYS

Unresolved anger toward father

ELIZABETH BARRETT BROWNING once wrote a sonnet in which she expressed the love she had for her husband Robert. The poem begins with the words, "How do I love thee? Let me count the ways." Inspired by these immortal words, I have thought about writing a similar poem about my father. A more appropriate opening to my poem would be, "How do I HATE thee? Let me count the ways." I would continue from there to write one of the longest poems in the history of literature. Each verse could start with a different reason for hating him. In verse one, I could expound on how frequently he comes home drunk and raises hell. Verse two could elaborate on his disgusting behavior while sober. Verse three could revolve around the fact that he keeps a disproportionate amount of his salary for himself at the expense of his family. After I wrote about two hundred verses, material for the poem would finally begin to run out.

My father's behavior has resulted in an extreme case of marital discord. I don't recall ever seeing my parents sleep together, nor have I seen them engage in kissing or any other form of mutual affection. For close to thirty years they have done nothing but argue and make home life an extremely anxiety-arousing situation. I never had to rival father for mother's love because in my lifetime he never had her love. Thus, modeling myself after father would not be conducive to gaining mother.

Marital discord has turned my siblings and myself into nervous wrecks. This nervousness is exemplified by the fact that I am continually engaged in either smoking, eating, or biting my fingernails. Some psychologists may argue that this behavior is a result of regression to the phase due to insufficient sucking during childhood. While this conclusion has validity and is undoubtedly a contributing factor, I believe that the presence of marital discord at home is the primary reason.

85

In this constant battle between my parents, I have without reservation taken the side of my mother. This is partially true because I blame most of the difficulties on my father and his drinking. Furthermore, my sympathies are with my mother because she is the weaker of the two. Dislike for father has also been fostered by the brain poisoning my mother has been subjecting me to in the past few years.

Everyone in my family hates my father. His behavior hastened the marriage of my brothers because they wanted to get away, as soon as possible, from the unhappy home life which he created. No member of the family talks to him unless it's absolutely necessary, and I don't remember initiating a conversation with him for at least a year. His questions are answered by "What do you care," "I don't know," or just "Don't bother me."

Conditions at home make it extremely hard to go to college. There is always the chance of divorce and ensuing economic disaster which would force me to quit school. Studying at home is nearly impossible because of the constant arguments and the general pain in the neck my father becomes when he is drunk. Oftentimes I have to wait for everyone to go to bed before I can start doing my homework. Thus the home becomes a place to eat and sleep, with the remainder of the time being spent in the library, the pool room, or just hanging around.

My present ambition is to kick my father's head in. Unfortunately, this ambition cannot be realized because I depend on him for support while I am going to college. I have sublimated my hostile feelings toward him by developing a fantasy in which I knock his block off. Accordingly, I propose that the first order of business on graduation day is to gently take off my father's glasses and then proceed to punch hell out of him. At age 68 perhaps my father won't be around long enough for me to accomplish my ambition, but, like my mother says, "Good people die every day but your father will probably live forever."

PEOPLE, PILLS, AND PUNCTURES

An over-stimulated, anxious, and guilty male

AS A SEVEN-POUND, two-ounce baby I was as normal as any other child. I grew in size normally and was walking at the age of eleven months. By the age of six months I had my first tooth. After conferring with my mother I found that I actually passed over the creeping stage and began walking. This evidently is the reason for my early ability to walk. My toilet training also began early and, as I am told, by a year and a half I was completely trained and kept my "pants dry." This I figure to be the reason for my concern for cleanliness.

I also remember being sent to bed without supper if I did not agree with what was served. This soon taught me that whether I liked what was given or not, it was better than nothing. My early manifestations of anger were tolerated to a certain degree. If I attempted a tantrum for attention or because I felt I had been wronged, it was accepted generally, as long as I kept it to a minimum. I can still remember sitting in the car alone for long periods of time because I was too stubborn to accept the responsibilities of my parents to visit relatives. This seclusion, I feel, was a good teacher.

Dependency is really a prime term in my life. From my earliest years, I was taught to be dependent on my parents for any needs which might arise. I feel, however, that this dependency grew too strongly, for it was quite a while before I began striving for independence. I noticed that my struggle for independence was frowned upon by my parents, who attempted to "keep me under their wing." I can remember many heated arguments.

My relations with my peers are varied. I have always been able to make friends rather easily and to keep these friends. I have found myself going out all hours of the night and doing many strange and foolish things for certain friends. It makes me wonder sometimes if I am foolish or not. Now I keep the number of close friends low and their friendship and faithfulness have been multiplied many times.

Since childhood I was always given the impression that sex was evil. I was never told anything of sex by my parents and I found myself being educated by my peers. This I believe is the cause of many of my problems. I began dating girls at a late age, fifteen. This was very different from the regular form of dating since the girl lived quite a distance away and I only saw her once every month or two and our affections toward each other were very mild.

My next association with females was with the girls in my neighborhood, some of whom have had illegitimate children, none of which are mine. I began to notice how the neighborhood gang had taken an important part in education of the neighborhood girls. About this time I found myself being driven by unconquerable urges for sexual satisfaction. These came from "petting to climax" at first. More and more I needed sex and at times I became uncontrollable. I would like to add at this point that I have never forced a girl into doing anything against her wishes and I have nothing but disgust for anyone doing this.

At seventeen I found myself getting strongly attached to an engaged girl. She sent her boy friend's ring back and I continued to see her for a period of nine months. During this time she had asked me for more than petting, but I could never bring myself to go any further. It was later that I knew that although I was "getting satisfied" she was not and this led to trouble which resulted in our breaking up.

Again I found myself seeing another man's girl. She too broke off with him and we began going together strongly. We thought of the future and had plans made for everything, which included marriage. Her former boy friend had treated her badly and would often beat her. I thought that if I were just the opposite and was kind to her, things would work out better. As time passed, she began taking advantage of me which led to our breaking off. Now things are unsettled and I am unsure as to what I should do. The main reason we broke up was because of her disapproval of being alone with me "parking." It was at such times that my sex urges became greatest and she knew it.

I have since met a girl who is quite oversexed and under-satisfied, and another girl who appeals to me very much. As I write this, I am in a quandary because today I have talked to all concerned. The absurd part of this is that I can't hold the idea of my girl going with someone else and she feels the same about me. It is for this reason that I feel we will go back.

To change the subject, I would like to tell you of a girl who lived a short distance from me for a time. She came from a broken home; her father is in California. This must be the reason for her behavior. She, never having had anyone who really cared for her, would treat all those in touch with her to having intercourse. She eventually got worse and became a nympho-maniac. There was no boy who could satisfy her needs and she lost interest in those who tried and failed. From this point, she turned to a Lesbian, hoping to find satisfaction. I can remember driving her girl friend home and seeing them carrying on in the back seat. This I think would shock quite a few as it did me. She has since been picked up on morals charges and placed on probation. She now lives in an apartment with another girl and I see very little of her. I must admit that I have had relations with her but add that I was interested in her in a different way. I had befriended her more out of sympathy than anything else because I believe that she is more ill and confused than she is bad. Even now if I could again contact her, I would attempt to help her.

In dealing with my means of getting rid of despair and dis-gust, I will say little. School, family problems, and social com-plications can weigh a person down quite badly. I used to turn to drinking sometimes and other times to certain pills. I would at times get so violent that I would begin to quiver all over. I may at times use a knife on myself and puncture my hands many times, not too deep, but enough to relieve tension. All kinds of ideas come into my head and I sometimes worry, not knowing what I am capable of doing.

OCTOPIA

Structuring a world to live in

ACCEPTANCE IN THE PEER GROUP is an important goal to social beings in every stage of life. College life with its pressures and constant strain requires an outlet to maintain an equilibrium between the tremendous tension and mental stability. The outlets available require contacts with peers in order to be accepted in their entertainment. Because acceptance is so important, college students I have witnessed constantly build a personality for themselves which the group will accept.

People in the group I have witnessed are typical of people in any group and fall into character types: the sexually aggressive, the mover, the quiet watch-out-for type, the lush, the tramp, the athlete, the timid, and the abused, for example. They type themselves by overcoming, through their manner of expression and action in the group, their own deficiencies which the group would not ordinarily accept.

The devout Catholic who has found her strict beliefs unacceptable to peer groups in the past will reflect a tough, hardened opinion against the beliefs of her past and conform to the accepted beliefs of the group. However, the extreme to which she will go to establish her acceptable opinion will reveal her real self. The raving on about the "ridiculous dogma" with arms waving and adjectives flying are all too indicative of a strong hidden guilt or conviction.

What is the group to me? The group molds, twists, and kneads one pliable until every action and expression has its encouraged and discouraged reaction from within, always with the attitudes of the group in mind. If I examine my feelings of hostility to the group (which is exactly how I feel), I would probably personify it and call it Parents, thwarted sex drives, responsibility, ambition to step on the next guy. If I were to multiply the group and give it a name I would call it society.

To my way of thinking, religion is an emotion. I firmly believe there has to be something good and pure and effective to
guide people in their interactions with other people in a complex
society. I find it very difficult to believe in religion as I see it in
the world today. The mere fact that there are many different
beliefs on many different subjects arouses doubt and creates a
feeling of distrust in firm orthodox religion. Some believe that
confession to a mortal being, as respresentative of God, can
remove guilt. I have no doubt that it does, but is it a God-
granted relief or a product of man's emotional make-up?

Since the beginning of time, villages, tribes, and civilizations
have had doubts about the causes of things. They have wondered
at the beauty of the heavens, the rotation of the earth, the
wonder of fire, and a million other wondrous things that were
unexplainable. These people we call primitive created gods to
answer their questions about the happenings of things in the
world in which they lived. Fire gods, gods of rain, snow, and
gods of every kind have been and still are created for man's
ignorance.

I am suggesting that man, because of his higher faculties of
the mind, is a wondering, a questioning, and a curious being
who, from the beginning of time, has sought answers to phe-
nomena.

At the time when a higher animal evolved to the point of
reason and had the ability to learn from experience, he solved
various problems for himself and left the rest for the gods to
answer. You may ask why did he turn here? What gave him the
idea of something supernatural? I have no concrete answers to
these questions and like any other questioning being can only
hypothesize.

Consider yourself one of the earliest men on a compara-
tively barren earth looking around you at the vastness of the
horizons. No matter what your vantage point is on the earth,
if you look around at the horizon, you are at the center of that
vast amount of land and space. I suggest that some time in later
stages of the development of reason you will have created a
vanity in yourself as a man because of your ability to master
your environment better than the lower animals. You will have
recognized that the master of animals and his environment is

man. I suggest that man had this vanity and any problem beyond his understanding he created a fear of or warmth for. This is superstition and out of superstition came gods. This was the genesis of religion.

Since that early beginning, man has answered more questions for himself and one by one has eliminated superstitions, and gods. One prominent example of this is to observe civilizations today and you will find that the more ignorant the man, the greater the prevalence of multideism. Throughout the evolution of man, his thought and his abilities have arrived at a world primarily of one God. Even today, however, there are less advanced societies with beliefs considered ridiculous in the light of our own more sophisticated beliefs.

I suggest that religions are a creation of a vain animal, a superstitious animal; yet the religious beliefs of this world are necessary to man. By what other means would he be kept sociable? If there were no religion today, vice, crime, and survival of the strong would be the rule of thumb in life.

I do suggest that religion is to me a belief in good and righteous behavior and variation from this behavior should arouse guilt. If one needs religion to create this knowledge of right and wrong and to relieve guilt, then he should have religion or whatever works for him. This is my belief in God and Religion.

Sex, Marriage, and Love are entities which our society attempts to organize into a healthy, acceptable expression within its own beliefs.

According to religious thought, marriage ceremonies grant sanction to the joining of two people into an acceptable union. Marriage ceremonies, according to my beliefs on religious matters, are a nice thing to have; yet through the passing of a day, society makes an about face and condones sex between man and woman.

Much literature and scientific research has been devoted to the study of the great discrepancy between sexual drives and social bans on the expression of those drives in acceptable activities. The audience to which I write is aware that this imbalance exists, so further explanation of it would be redundant; however, I would like to give my opinion on a very apparent trend that is taking place.

The great trend toward rebellion and especially against the sex taboos of society are caused because of greater aggressive tendencies. These tendencies are a result of pushing younger people to strive further in activities involving the intellect, and this I believe is the immediate cause of the rebellion and open aggression and expression of sex.

This generation more than the last, and the next generation more than this one, will be less satisfied with long walks and quiet, simple physical exertions which seemed to release tension in the early 1900's. The daily activities of our grandfathers included perhaps ten hours of hard work releasing physical tension and aggression. The daily activities of today are spent more often in sitting, thinking, being sociable, and other activities involving tension and expressions of the mind, not the body.

Wild parties, delinquent gang fights, breaking windows, and murder are extreme expressions of aggression, but the quiet, subtle aggressions of those who are more intelligent of the consequences of spontaneous aggression will release their aggression in sex.

I have no doubt at all that the trend in sexual expression will increase and the present generation of adolescents will render sex more acceptable, apart from the consideration of marriage, than the older generation of today.

As sure as I am that marriage and sex are exclusive, I am just as sure that love and marriage are inclusive. Marriage is only a ceremony to me, and the word has come to express a union between two who love each other. I will attempt to get away from the use of the word marriage by explaining what I believe it involves and will have to contain in order for me to consider it for myself.

It should be a psychological lift for both the man and woman. Each should have enough strength in areas the other is weak in to make a strong tie and a working partnership. Their ambitions should be equal, and they should want the same things out of life and marriage. They should be sexually satisfied with each other and know this before marriage. Each should have respect for the other and respond with encouragement in areas of the other's weaknesses. As a quick check to see if two people are compatible, they should ask themselves if they like the person without regard for love, and if the other qualities I have mentioned are intact, this can be called love.

That no man is an island is a terrible shame; that there are no Walden Ponds left far enough away from life is a reminder that the world is too crowded; that man is a dependent, sociable animal is a reminder of the stagnant situation he has multiplied to and can never change without annihilating his fellow man or doing without the pleasures of children.

The Octopus has grown from a small, wandering animal to a confining multi-armed beast grasping and twisting everyone and everything into shape. Its arms, each with its purpose, reach out and remind us of what he will and won't allow us to do, and when we overstep our bounds, he slaps us down and swats us back into shape.

The central system of society has taken over our minds and infiltrated our reason, causing us to think our way into confining ways of life.

One arm of Octopia pushes us through school and college to strive ahead and be better than the next guy. It kneads us into a "professional" to be looked up to by the innocent who are not yet a working cog in the survival of the fittest world.

Arm number two is Parental Ambition. Parents sitting on the shoulder of Octopia push the buttons that regulate the grasp on their children, opening and closing according to their ideas of right and wrong which are subject to their prejudices.

Arm three is Peer Acceptance, a relaxed muscle, who pushes gently always ready to throw you back to loneliness with a hidden strength and explosiveness if its requirements are not lived up to.

Arms four and five are called Masculine Grasp and Feminine Grasp, respectively. They are located very close to each other with each grasping the genitals of the other. The victims in grasp are allowed to hold hands, and even embrace, as they reach each to each from within the fist. When biological drives make known their need, Octopia squeezes, sending pangs of condemnation and guilt throughout the body.

Arm six, the shaking nervous arm of Responsibility, taps his fingers loudly as a constant reminder that racks the brain and keeps the other arms moving in untiring motions to keep Octopia what it is.

7   Arm seven, beautiful arm seven, lies at the top of Octopia. It is dead. The fist lies open, and the people are running out and expressing themselves; pure uncontrolled expressions of inner desires and pent-up intentions flee, leaving smiles on their faces and a peace in their hearts. They are fortunate enough to have the speed and will power to avoid the grasp of all the other restraining limbs.

8   Arm eight is the auxiliary force that roves throughout the country and offers additional strength where Octopia may temporarily weaken.

DOINGS

IN THIS PAPER I plan to explain some of the actions of an adolescent gang or group (whichever you wish to call them). This group ranges from 17 to 19 years of age. These adolescents (including myself) have been around each other for seven years. Although now I am not around them as much as I used to be (about two or three years ago I would have considered myself an active member), I still hang around with them every once in a while. Because of the length of my association with this gang, I believe that I know it fairly well.

First of all, let me tell you a little about each of its primary members. The first member, Buff, is the probable leader because most of the kids usually find out what he is going to do before they plan to do anything. The reason for his popularity is because of his relatively pleasant, fun-loving attitude; besides, most of the good times usually have involved him.

Tim is slightly taller than most of the gang (around six feet two inches); although he is well-liked, he has an explosive temper.

Mike's father died in the war. He already has a scholarship set aside for him if he wishes to go to college. He has been told that he has a very high I.Q. During grade school (grades one through nine) he received mostly A's and B's without any work; however, in high school he has frequently quit school entirely.

Bill is a five foot six inch punkish-looking kid. By punkish I mean he even looks like a typical juvenile delinquent. You know what I mean, the long sideburns, etc.

I believe the factor that brought these kids together was the need for activity (excitement). At one time or another, there were more kids in this gang, but I noticed that whenever a kid finished his association with the gang (by this I mean he was still on friendly terms, but he was no longer an active factor in the gang), he no longer went in for the mischief that characterized the gang.

Through the early adolescent years, the gang's mischief consisted mostly of being in places and taking things that did not belong to us. For instance, playing in new houses under construction, using a cemetery as a playground, even though the police were frequently summoned to expel us, and hanging around old deserted buildings. Some of the things we took were materials for huts, or projects as cement tubs (industry used these to mix cement or chemicals in) which we used for boats. We might light fires in a field to clear it for a baseball field. Now this can be a sign of mischief, but then again most of these boys came from parents who had to work hard for their achievements.

Bill comes from the poorest family of the group, and the only time he ever got something he could use was when it benefited the family. Buff only received an allowance when his father sold a car (his father was an automobile dealer); also we always kidded him about how his father would always spend more money on the old car rather than buy a new one, and these cars used to really fall apart.

Although not everyone was willing to go along with the reason why we did something, everyone would go along just for the excitement. In looking for an explanation, I would say that we were just satisfying our want for things that might have been denied us. I believe we got our satisfaction from the fact that we were preventing someone from keeping something away from us. In short, you might say we were going against the limitations that our elders had imposed on us.

Now let me discuss aggression. During our youthful years (early adolescence) we were always active (a quest for excitement). We got rid of most of our aggression during this time through our participation in sports, for just about every one of us was active in sports (the school team). When we were not playing among ourselves, we were always challenging other groups. (We usually always won.) As the years passed, our activities changed from outlets in sports to betting (cards, pool, etc.). Once again, however, this was characterized by fervent participation.

Once we reached high school, a change took place; since our physical activity had been more subdued, we indulged in more violent acts that just didn't make sense. Some examples were: breaking into a country club to steal four hundred dollars worth of booze; stealing one thousand dollars worth of golf equipment from another country club; often waiting for a truck carrying beer to stop for a delivery, then stealing the cases from the back of the truck; looting parking meters. Although we were not really tough guys, quite often one of the gang would deliberately pick a fight with someone who was much bigger than he.

I believe that this aggression is a replacement for the activity in the early years and a replacement for the participation in sports. Now as for the explanation for the need for activity, the reasons are probably many. We identified with a role that was too active. Thus in a sense you might say our fantasies became too much of a reality.

Buff, who in his earlier years was one of the kids who did it just for the excitement, has become more intensely identified with the gang. He is an intense gambler and is always ready to participate in a gang fight. At this moment his record reads: drunkenness, disturbing the peace, grand larceny. At this moment he is standing trial for breaking and entering and larceny. This is a good example of his gang identification in that he went along with two other kids' idea to rob a college dormitory.

Tim is now in the army. He was kicked out of the high school basketball team for arguing with the coach (maybe the coach represents parental discipline). He is the one who usually started most of the fights.

Mike has quit school and is standing trial for stealing a car and trying to run a police blockade. Although in the early years he was mild in his participation with the gang, since quitting school he has now developed the "buddy" attitude. By this I mean if my buddies are in a fight, it's my duty to help them; if my buddy is going to do this, I will too, etc. I think the gang is serving the purpose of his dead father; thus his male role identification is with the gang.

Bill right now is engaged to be married and you would no

longer consider him an active member. He is different from the rest of the members in that he comes from a large family. He is the second oldest; the oldest was a sister who got married before she finished high school. Even in his early adolescence he was the "show-off," the "wise guy"; he is always the one who will do something foolish. Although he never participates in gang fights, when he is picked on he always has to have a weapon. He was the first one to have a car and he makes good use of it. Another characteristic of his is that he is probably the heaviest drinker in the crowd. He is an attention-getter because of his unimportance in the family (since the youngest always gets the most attention). His excessive drinking, his need for a weapon when in a fight, and his use of a car are the ways that he proves that he is a man. Another thing to remember is, as I have already mentioned, he is relatively small in size and therefore is probably self-conscious.

WEARING BLINDFOLDS

"What if she decides she loves the other guy?"

ALTHOUGH the ethnic environment in my life has come from two directions, I tend to lean toward the Mexican. I grew up overly conscious of the need to belong to the group. While I was accepted, I was fine; but if I lost that bond, my deep insecurities flowed out.

I had always hung around with an older group; even now I do. When I was 12 years old the other boys in my group were 14 or 15 and in my neighborhood I was exposed to girls who were 13–15 years old. At this time I had my first experience with a girl, who was 14 or 15. Although I didn't know what to do, she showed me the ropes and since she knew "everything", I felt safe when she told me that since I wasn't circumcised, she couldn't get pregnant. This experience leads me to believe that most children from my area up to 15–18 years old or older are wearing blindfolds.

This is one reason why so many girls are taken advantage of so early in life. After my "experience", I was still afraid of sexuality, while at the same time desiring it. These early experiences started desires which became chain reactions leading me into the wild crowd in high school where we had freedom of expression in wild parties, drinking, and petting. Most of my high school contacts were informal in that I didn't go steady with any one girl but played the field.

The main point of this discussion is to selfishly explore my feelings and adequacies concerning one main area of my life in recent years.

I met Ann in the ninth grade when we became next door neighbors. She was hanging around with an older group because of her physical development. I envied the boys who went out with her but I was afraid of her in some way. I can't remember why.

I never knew Ann very well until my senior year. We were attracted to each other at a party and started a weekly date. We engaged in heavy petting until one night she made an offer. I turned it down because I thought I loved her and she had been hurt before by other guys, and I didn't want her to think I was out for what I could get. Before, I had always taken as much as I could. All the talk about proving masculinity to ourselves is true enough but our social mores make it work both ways. If you act in a way to prove it to yourself, you are also many times proving it to your peers and isn't this the main idea of our self-centered culture?

As it turned out, Ann started playing the field again and we broke up over this. During the following months I paid as little attention to her as possible because "women don't love men who show their love." Everyone has to play the big game, cat and mouse; and put a big wall up around ourselves. If you come out of your shell with the wrong person you can be crushed.

When Ann saw me with a girl from high school who was very popular, she was green with envy and tried to get my affections back. We made plans to meet at a Ski Lodge where everyone was going. The first night I was with Mary but when Ann came to me I told Mary to leave and Ann slept with me that night but we didn't make love.

Later we made love quite frequently, and I was on cloud nine. I had never had relations with a girl I was in love with and my fulfilment was complete, as was hers.

When I went back to school we started drifting apart and I realized that she was unsure of her love for me. She told me that she had been thinking lately about a guy she used to go out with and always loved until she met me. This guy had everything she ever wanted. He was rich, blond, extremely good looking, and a nice guy besides.

Now I am the type that hates to admit that anyone is a nicer guy or better looking than I am. I suppose I am extremely vain but I am good looking and although I am not a rugged type I have been told by girls that I am very sexy and attractive. This is very important because I do not consider myself a wit, an intellect, or the life of the party.

I was completely detached from school. Ann was on my mind constantly. I decided not to show any affection towards her but she kept calling me. Finally I went out with her and everything went back the way it was. She showed her love for me while still professing an attraction for this other guy. This is where the conflict arises. How can I deny my love when she says that she wants me but has to get this man out of her mind first?

Are my actions inconsistent with the masculine role in our society? I want to show Ann that I am a real man but I love her so much that when I am near her I want to do things for her. It's a shame that we are so often not accepted for what we are but must strive to build a facade of false social fronts in order to attain certain goals.

My problem is that Ann, a beautiful girl with a tremendous charm, has almost every interest common with mine. All I must do to have her for my own is to treat her harshly and she will come to me, for she wants a man who will dominate her.

I have been brought up in a house that is ultimately run by my father but is pervaded by a common interest council which makes most of the decisions. What I mean is that my father takes into consideration opinions set forth by my mother. This makes me feel that I will be inclined to have the same liberal attitude with my wife. But won't I be able to enforce ideals that I have acquired more recently than in the first five years of my life when supposedly much of my personality was formed? I hope so for it seems a shame, even if true, that a person's personality is largely formed before he knows the score. If this is true maybe we can form a perfect society some day by having young children live in a simulated society set up to produce the model citizen; instead of allowing these souls to be exposed to dedicated yet perverted parents and teachers who may sway the child to false values in our society.

How can I love a girl who loves another man and feel satisfied when I am with her and dejected when I am not? I worry about her welfare and feel that I have helped her to beware of sexuality in the wrong circumstances. How could a girl be so blind as to fall for lines and false pretenses. The problem is whether people care or not. So many people just don't care and if no one cares and you are not a self-sufficient person, life isn't worth much except to satisfy someone else physically or spiritually. If self respect is lost, all hope of success is gone.

Now I realize that perhaps I must forget Ann for even if I love her, I will not look forward to a life with a woman who is not sure of her affections. It may be the same for her whole life and what if she decides that she loves the other guy?

ESCAPE INTO LONELINESS

Fantasy is easier than life

I CAN REMEMBER when I was young enough to want to sleep with my parents. I always felt uneasy when I was sleeping with both parents but when my father left I felt more at ease. I can remember wanting to get closer to my mother only when my father left. At times she would move and I could feel how soft and warm she was, and I wanted to get closer to her but I cannot remember ever doing this. Maybe this is why I am not as close to her now to talk to as I wish.

I do not remember too much of my earlier life except that I could always seem to get around my mother, but not my father. I believe this had a definite effect on my later life and I will explain this later.

The deepest and most lasting impression made upon me by my parents was when I was in sixth grade. My older brother was then in the tenth grade. A girl called him up on the phone and asked him to a dance. When my mother found out about this, there was a big argument in the house. My mother called the girl back and told her that it was not proper for a girl to call a boy. I cried all night because I was worrying what the kids in school would say the next day.

From then on, until my graduation from high school, I was afraid to speak to girls. I knew that if they got to like me, then they might call and another argument might come.

When I was in the seventh grade, I met a girl that I liked. One day she came to my house. Now I really became scared: If my mother ever saw me with a girl, then she would really get mad. Because of this fear, I chased the girl away and she never came back.

Another time, and with a different girl, the same thing happened. She told my friend that she liked me and was going to call me. Immediately I began to panic, so I told her that if *I* liked her, *I* would call her. I never called her and I was relieved when I came home and she didn't call.

As I am writing this, things seem to fit together for the first time. Now I can plainly see how early incidents can influence a person for years. I believe this to be one of the reasons I was so shy in school. That phone call made a deep and lasting impression on me. I also believe this incident to have had a remarkable effect on me when I was in high school.

I know that another reason for my being so shy was the fact that I had acne. I would think of this all the time and I envied anyone with a clear skin. If anyone talked in front of me about acne, I would get nervous and scared. I was so self-conscious that when talking to a person, I always kept my head down. I was brought to a point where I felt inferior to other people.

In high school, I was also very awkward. I had identified myself with people in athletics. I read stories about Lou Gehrig, Mickey Mantle, Yogi Berra, and Rocky Graziano. All these athletes were good at sports, but very awkward and shy when it came to girls. If these men could gain social acceptance without having girls like them, then why couldn't I? I was a fairly good athlete, so I decided to try to become better and also pattern my life after these men. Since I was eleven years old, I would pray every night to become a professional ballplayer.

At that time, I heard a minister talk about baseball players. He said the difference between the man who started and the one on the bench was the fact that one asked God's help. When I got to high school, basketball was my favorite sport. I would count the days until the first day of practice. I brought rubber balls to school and sometimes during class I would squeeze them to get stronger wrists. When I got home, I would take a ball and work with it till I was sore. At night I would dream of making great plays. Everything I did was directed toward my ultimate goal of becoming a professional player. I knew that if I was to become one I would have to at least make the varsity my freshman year. I didn't make it, and I was worried and became disappointed; I would worry all the time. Maybe I was worrying because I wanted to prove to myself that there was a God. I knew that if someone like me could become a professional player, then only someone with great powers could bring this about.

When I became a junior, I knew I could make the varsity but I was still worried. I made the team, but did poorly. But I thought at least here was a bit of a start.

My senior year I expected big things of myself. Each night I prayed to do well in games, but each day I did badly. At night I would cry because I knew that I would never make all-scholastic. All my prayers seemed to be wasted. I felt as though God had let me down.

I feel that the reason was because of my inferiority feelings and complete dependence on my parents. When I played base-ball I would feel it was the pitcher against the batter. One man against one other. It was I who usually lost this battle. I also wrestled in high school, but I never won a match. One could say I was just a bad wrestler, but this was not the real reason. I know that when I stepped onto the mat, I felt inferior to my opponent and anxious. Here again, in a situation with one opponent versus just one other, I lost every match. When I played football, it was the same story. Here is a sport where eleven men work together. I had plenty of confidence in football, especially when I was carrying the ball, because the other men were there blocking for me. I was dependent on the other men, but there was always one thing I feared going into games. I was always afraid of having a man coming down the field and having just me between him and a touchdown. Again here is a situation where one man is against just one other, and it was this that I was always afraid of. In this situation, no one could help me. In hitting, no one could help me and in wrestling, no one could help me. Here are three situations where I was all alone and it was this that I feared.

The wanting to become a professional athlete definitely affected my life. I wanted to make all-scholastic so much, but I failed and when I knew I would never make it, I almost went out of my mind with worry. This is why I do not have any real goals in sports any more. I may play them but I never set a high goal for myself. If I did, and failed, I would go through the same agony over again. Maybe this will keep me from becoming a better athlete and maybe people will call me a coward, but I know worrying does not do any good. I will just do the best I can and if I do well, then fine; but if I don't, the world will still go on spinning.

Because of my acne, and my parents' restrictive attitude toward girls, I was in sort of a bind. During the weekends, most of my friends were out on dates, but I was alone. I was afraid to meet girls because of my skin and my parents. At times, I would just sit in the dark and think. I wanted to be with people so much, but I was all alone. Then I would start thinking of a girl that was pretty. Even if she didn't like me, I pretended that she did and that she was my girlfriend. Like a child, I was living in a dream world. Physically I was sixteen years old, but acting childish. I remember holding my stomach and feeling nauseous. I felt empty and alone. Perhaps the only thing that would keep me from being lonely was a girl, but I was afraid of girls, and if I did have a girlfriend, my parents would be mad. So I had an imaginary girl. For a year or more, I had God's mother as my imaginary girl. This sounds stupid and confusing, so I will explain.

In the Catholic religion, God's mother is also called Mary or the Blessed Lady. I would always read stories about Her. One saint to whom She appeared said that She looked so beautiful and about sixteen or seventeen years old. I was always taught that She was very kind and understanding. What more could I ask for in a girl. If anyone could understand me and comfort me, it was Her. If She is all I was taught, She wouldn't care how I looked.

I remember that my father was always very strict about things but if I wanted anything, I could get around my mother. Many times my mother would talk to my father and I would get what I wanted. This could be the reason why whenever I prayed, I would always ask Mary's help. I would always go to Her first. Now that I am writing, I am also thinking. I know that I always wanted to be close to the Blessed Lady. Maybe in reality what I was doing was saying, "I want so much to be close to my mother, but I'm not really." I was taught also that Mary was our real mother and God was our real father. Because I was not as close to my mother as I wished, I made the Blessed Lady my real mother and tried to get as close to Her as I could.

At times, I could talk about things that were close to me to my mother, but never to my father. Maybe this is why when I prayed, I very rarely asked God's help directly. I would always pray to the Blessed Lady to ask God for me.

Now that I had an imaginary girl, I felt a little better. I had a girl that my parents would never know about, and one that didn't care how I looked. It helped for a while, but I still got lonely. There were times when I remember praying to see Her because I wanted something real, something alive. Most of all, I wanted someone to talk to and someone to talk to me. But this never happened. I never did see Her. I thought of Her a lot and what She must look like, but I never saw Her. I figured the next best thing to do was to paint a picture of what I thought She looked like. I spent hours trying to paint the kindest and most understanding face I could. These were the qualities that I wanted in a girl and this is what I needed most. If I went to my parents, I would have gotten some, but not as much as I wanted. I would not go to them anyway, because I felt they wouldn't understand and I also had too much pride. Maybe this pride stems back to my early childhood when I wanted so much to be close to my mother in bed, but I would not give in. I would not go to her.

When I was not painting, I was writing about Mary. I tried to put my loneliness to some practical use. I wanted other people that were lonely to see what I had painted. Maybe they, too, could feel a little less lonely. I wanted to express my innermost thoughts and desires in a picture, in words, or in any way I could. I also wanted to show people how kind and beautiful the Mother of God really is. It was not beauty like the girls in Hollywood have. It was beauty of heart and soul that would far exceed any woman in the world.

This has affected my life in many ways. I am always praying to Her and sometimes I still feel that I could never really love a girl because I will be thinking of the Blessed Lady as my girl. The first girl I told I loved was a girl that was in a convent for three years. She came out and we started to date. Maybe I was looking for something in her that I saw in my imaginary girl-friend.

I do know where I want to go in life and why. I want to work with children. My parents very rarely sat down and talked to me. My father hardly ever spoke to me unless it was about gardening which is his work. He is very quiet. Sometimes my mother talks to me and when she does, I love her so much. Usually she just yells and lectures like most mothers. If only they could try to understand me and listen to what I have to say without lecturing. If I could only once leave the house without their saying a hundred times, "Watch out driving," or "Don't be in late," I could love them so much more. I'd feel so much better if once they would just say, "Have a good time."

I always wanted my parents to talk to me about what I thought of most of the time and what I wanted to be in life. I remember once talking to my mother about something that was very close to me. She listened for a while and I loved her so much, but then she said I was crazy to think like I did. That really hurt me, because it meant so much to me to have her understand. I wanted to tell somebody about my problems and how I thought so I went to a priest. Priests were always kind. One priest in particular I remember best. He understood everything I said. He was so kind and understanding that I decided I wanted to return this kindness and understanding to children who need it. This is the reason I want to work with children. If God wants, this is one goal I will achieve.

I have always wanted to express my innermost and deepest feelings whether it be painting, writing or just plain talking. With children, I will be able to express my deepest and innermost feeling—love.

If I am with children, I know I will have a tough time, but there will be moments when they will want me to listen to their innermost thoughts and dreams in life. It will be in these brief but very precious moments that I will have returned the kindness and understanding that was given me.

It will be here that I will not be alone anymore. As long as I have people around, I am happy.

THE NEW MEMBER

Sibling rivalry

I DON'T THINK I can interpret my own behavior, but being able to look at incidents which have impressed me allows me to study it with some understanding. Truthfully, I don't feel that I have the amount of knowledge to be sure of my interpretations of any behavior, but perhaps this feeling is, to some extent, a defense to insure that I don't learn too much about myself.

My own family consists of my mother, father, and one younger brother. I really don't know what makes my parents "tick" because, so to speak, I am too close to the forest to see the trees. My father seems to be characterized by relative submission to and resentment of authority, and a tendency to be prejudiced. This seems to fit with the impression I have that *his* father was very authoritarian. My mother seems much more independent in her actions and in some ways seems to rebel against authority. Some of this independence is evident in my behavior.

I was three years of age when my brother was born, and I can agree that the birth of a second child may have a detrimental effect upon the first. Looking back, I recall an incident which occurred when I was about four years old. When I heard my mother calling my brother's name, I rushed in from another room and clung to her skirt. She immediately told me to stop being "jealous." Now, I am sure I had no idea of the meaning of the word "jealous," but I can remember experiencing an immediate and intense feeling of guilt, so I must have known what she was referring to. This incident stands out above all others that I can readily recall during my preschool years and although I might be wrong, I think the birth of my brother has greatly affected my personality. Before my mother had verbalized my exact feelings that day, I was vaguely aware of something that made me feel as though I had to compete with the new member of the family for attention and affection. Although I was allowed to hold the baby and help to dress and feed him, I still felt left out of something—he was the object of attention, not me—I only helped to give HIM attention. This blow to my emerging self concept, this intruder called "the baby" was what I had been a few years earlier. How could I have ever been like him, I wondered, and besides, I was quick to notice, he possessed something which I didn't. Maybe I felt that he was more or less the object of attention because of this something which I lacked.

At any rate, my guilt feelings seem to have manifested themselves in a feeling of inferiority which I can recall vividly during my early school years, and less vividly, though I was still aware of it, as I grew older. I can remember being very critical of my looks, and when I was six years old, the idea came to me that as soon as I was old enough I would pluck my eyebrows like my mother did so that I wouldn't be so awful to look at. On the first day of school, I was startled by the fact that three walls of the classroom were covered with blackboards, which when I faced them, gave the feeling that the walls were going to close in and crush me. Even now I have a tendency to fear small closed-in places and this might be an outgrowth of my guilt over feelings of jealousy—the idea that I am going to be punished for feeling this way.

I excelled in school work and was often in command of a group. My striving for excellence might have been an attempt to rid myself of feelings of inferiority. During these years I developed a need to cultivate a primary relationship with a peer. I was usually successful at this, and when our ways parted, I would establish a similar relationship with someone else, never feeling really complete when this person was not around. Attempts to prove myself not inferior are related to the fact that I could out-run, out-climb, and out-fight any boy in the neighborhood, not to speak of the girls.

With the onset of adolescence I experienced the usual difficulties, a new self image and the desire for increased independence. My high school years were not abnormally difficult, however, and I surrounded myself with a group of girl friends and I always had one very close friend. What stands out during these years is the attitude with which I began to regard my studies. The desire for excellence was still there but I decided that I couldn't be bothered exerting the effort required to achieve the highest grades. I had the ability, I felt, but I was lazy. I was still able to compete, especially with males, but holding myself back was a way of punishing myself in order to alleviate the guilt stemming from jealousy of my brother. At fifteen I decided I would like to make a career in economics. By devoting myself to establishing a career I would be able to compete in what I already saw as a man's world. As time went on, however, the idea of devoting my life to a career seemed more unrealistic.

At sixteen I started to work in a department store. One of my closest friends worked there but we seldom saw each other, and so I was alone, especially at break time, with people I had never met before, some my age, but most a rowdy group of older women. It was at this time that I started smoking. That was a miserable experience as I often nearly choked, and many were the times I had to rest my head on the table pretending to have a headache because I didn't want anyone to see my smoke-filled eyes watering. And still I persisted, because although it required using half a book of matches to get the thing lit, I could experience a feeling of completeness in the midst of all these strangers. (I still don't really enjoy smoking, but the idea of breaking the "habit" is one I rarely think of).

My feelings of inferiority seem much less intense now, perhaps because they are more hidden. Some of the feeling is hidden behind a defensive attitude of indifference. My academic mediocrity might be a way of letting myself "have my cake and eat it too". Supposedly performing below capacity in some subjects is a way of punishing myself but I will still obtain a college education which will allow me to feel somewhat superior. Then with marriage, hopefully, will come the permanent sense of completeness.

Although my brother and I are not extremely close, our relationship is a fairly good one. Now almost fifteen, he is living proof of much that has been said to characterize adolescence. First and foremost, he is a man, and if one is doubtful, the three whiskers on his chin will bear testimony to the fact. When

I asked him what animal he would most like to be, he replied, with some embarrassment, "The most playful animal, like a lion cub." This might be a reflection of conflicting desires to remain dependent and become independent. His actions are of interest to me because I passed through a similar stage not so very long ago. I am no longer aware of jealous feelings toward him, either they no longer exist or they have been hidden.

That his arrival has had an effect on my personality I have little doubt, but there are other aspects of my behavior that I am unable or unwilling to admit to or examine. Now that I have written this brief paper, I feel somewhat like a traitor to myself, but the thought has occurred to me that my reasons for writing about myself given at the beginning of the paper are just rationalizations. Perhaps admitting my guilt to the outside is another way of delivering myself for punishment.

NOEL